BE A SUCCESS MAVERICK

How Ordinary People
Do It Different
to Achieve Extraordinary Results

Published by
The Maverick Millionaire Publishing
New York, NY

Manufactured in the United States of America, or in the United Kingdom when distributed elsewhere.

Finck, Paul
    Be a Success Maverick : How Ordinary People Do It Different to
Achieve Extraordinary Results
LCCN: 2017959818
ISBN: 978-0-9996381-5-6
e Book: 978-0-9996381-4-9

Cover design: Joe Potter
Copyediting: Claudia Volkman
Interior design: Claudia Volkman
Maverick Millionaire Logo Design: Joe Potter

www.BeASuccessMaverick.com
www.TheMaverickMillionairePublishing.com

PHOTO CREDITS

Anthony Patrick: Milo Cross
Benjamin Chatson: Sam Diaz
Brenda and Don Hayward: Elicia Schopfer
Bridget Brady: Bridget Brady
Deirdre Virvo: Tendai Gomo
Drew Berman: Drew Berman
Julie Cotton: Jason Michael Hammond
Keith Meals: Paul Finck
Kelly Carter: Danny Pesta
Ken and Barbara Tomayko: Ken and Barbara Tomayko
Kevin Vibert: Janet Frick
Mark Yuzuik: Mark Yuzuik
Matt Brauning: The Mendoza Agency
Patrick Kluge: Scott Felson
Paul Brown: Jordan Lee
Paul Finck: Adam Sternberg
Paul Wilkins: Leticia Wilkins
Reggie Brooks: Keith Hamilton
Sam Garwood: Danny Pesta
Sinéad Sanderson: Brian Tomayko
Teresa R. Martin, ESQ: Blue Artists, LLC

TABLE OF CONTENTS

Introduction   ix

My First Maverick Moments, *Paul Finck*   1

The Big "Break": What You Think, You Get, *Keith Meals*   7

The Power of Passion, *Mark Yuzuik*   11

Three Secrets to Align Your Mind to Win, *Matt Brauning*   15

How to Sell Before You Finish Your Rehab, *Reggie Brooks*   19

Honor. Sanctitude. Resilience. *Kelly Carter*   23

The HVAC Marketing Wheel Reinvented, *Sam Garwood*   27

Becoming a Marketplace Whisperer, *Bridget Brady*   31

Living the Laptop Lifestyle, *Drew Berman*   35

Living the American Dream, *Anthony Patrick*   39

It's Never Too Late, *Ken and Barb Tomayko*   43

Change the Game, *Paul Brown*   47

Improv as a Spiritual Practice, *Julie Cotton*   51

Probate 101 for Real Estate Investors, *Paul Wilkins*   55

Get Up, Dress Up, Show Up, and Never Give Up, *Sinéad Sanderson*   59

Rocketman–Pedaling to Paradise, *Kevin Vibert*   63

Rad Ways, *Patrick Kluge*   67

God Is My Real Estate Agent, *Brenda Hayward*   71

Universal Sales Hacks, *Benjamin Chatson*   75

Work It! *Deirdre Virvo*   79

From Financial Ruin to Business Success, *Dr. Teresa R. Martin, ESQ*   83

DEDICATION

As I strive to be a role model, leader, mentor, coach, teacher, trainer, and all that will be me on my road to reaching my fullest potential, I am thankful to everyone who has been all these things and more to me. Before you is the manifestation, resulting from great passion, joy, effort, commitment, perseverance, and desire; yet, it is ONLY with all your love and support that I am able to bring this great work to life.

I want to thank my wife, Deborah Finck, for being by my side unconditionally throughout this amazing journey of life. She is my inspiration, my motivation, and my soul mate, now and forever.

I want to thank my children, Amanda, Alexandra, Stephen, Katerina, David, and Daniel, for being amazing role models. Your collective strength of character and your inspirational presence during both the hard times and glorious times make me so proud to be called your father.

I want to thank each and every one of you who have meant so much to me in my continuous journey. To name even a few would not do you justice; there have been so many that have touched my life and my heart. Know you are loved and remembered. Thank you!

INTRODUCTION

Maverick is defined as "someone who refuses to play by the rules. He/she isn't scared to cross the line of conformity." As a matter of fact, Mavericks tend to write their own rule book.

Mavericks of our day are all around us. We admire them for their courage and marvel at their success. We idolize them as all-knowing and admonish them for the bold actions they take. Most of all we want to understand what makes them tick.

Some of our modern-day Mavericks include the likes of:

Steve Jobs (Apple)
Anita Roddick (The Body Shop)
Jack Welch (General Electric)
Guy Laliberté (Cirque du Soleil)
Mark Zuckerberg (Facebook)
Bill Gates (Microsoft)
Richard Branson (Virgin)
Arianna Huffington (The Huffington Post)
Donald Trump (President)

Everyone of these people created massive change in their field by looking at things differently, acting differently, and doing things differently than anyone else. As Mavericks, they created massive success by recreating their industry. This is what Mavericks do best. Mavericks reinvent, redesign, reanalyze, reconnect . . . they rework everything around them and end up creating something new, different, exciting—Inspiring and Amazing!

In this book, I am proud to share with you stories of ordinary people who "Do It Different" to achieve extraordinary results and have stepped into the whelm of Mavericks in their own right. Each and every one of them has created amazing success in their life by doing things different and finding their own unique path to greatness. My prayer for you is that this book inspires you to do the same: to reach for the stars in your own unique wonderful way and create your own path to reach your fullest potential.

THIS BOOK COMES ALIVE WITH REVEALIO — Augmented Reality Marketing Mobile App. Check out the live introductory video on the cover of this book. Follow these simple steps and be ready to be amazed by connecting the Maverick Way™.

1. Download the "Revealio — AR Marketing Mobile App."
2. Select "View a Revealio" from the home screen in the mobile app.
3. Hold your phone over front of this book.
4. Watch as the book comes alive and enjoy the short video.

To get us started on our journey together, here are some amazing quotes from other Mavericks throughout time. Enjoy!

Your faithful Guide
Paul Finck
The Maverick Millionaire®

"Do It Different. Be a Maverick"
Paul Finck

"In order to be irreplaceable one must always be different."
Coco Chanel

"If there's any message to my work, it is ultimately that it's OK
to be different, that it's good to be different, that we should question ourselves
before we pass judgment on someone who looks different, behaves different,
talks different, is a different color."
Johnny Depp

"The person who follows the crowd will usually go no further than the crowd. The
person who walks alone is likely to find himself
in places no one has ever seen before."
Albert Einstein

"Be daring, be different, be impractical, be anything that will assert integrity of purpose and imaginative vision against the play-it-safers, the creatures of the commonplace, the slaves of the ordinary."
Cecil Beaton

"To be nobody but yourself in a world doing its best to make you everybody else means to fight the hardest battle any human can ever fight and never stop fighting."
E. E. Cummings

"Always be a first rate version of yourself, instead of a second rate version of somebody else."
Judy Garland

"Be who you are and say what you feel, because those who mind don't matter and those who matter don't mind."
Dr. Seuss

"Keep away from people who belittle your ambitions. Small people always do that, but the really great make you feel that you, too, can become great."
Mark Twain

"Only those who will risk going too far can possibly find out how far one can go."
T. S. Eliot

"I took the one less traveled by, and that has made all the difference."
Robert Frost

"If you do what you've always done, you'll get what you've always gotten."
Tony Robbins

"If you're offered a seat on a rocket ship, don't ask what seat! Just get on."
Sheryl Sandberg

"If you're going to be thinking anything, you might as well think big."
Donald Trump

"Man cannot discover new oceans unless he has the courage to lose sight of the shore."
Andre Gide

"If you do things well, do them better. Be daring, be first, be different, be just."
Anita Roddick (The Body Shop)

"You can't outwit fate by trying to stand on the sidelines and place little side bets about the outcome of life. Either you wade in and risk everything to play the game, or you don't play at all. And if you don't play, you can't win."
Judith McNaught

"If things seem under control, you are just not going fast enough."
Mario Andretti

"Do the one thing you think you cannot do. Fail at it. Try again. Do better the second time. The only people who never tumble are those who never mount the high wire. This is your moment. Own it."
Oprah Winfrey

"Life is inherently risky. There is only one big risk you should avoid at all costs, and that is the risk of doing nothing."
Denis Waitley

"Your time is limited, so don't waste it living someone else's life."
Steve Jobs

"If you are not willing to risk the unusual,
you will have to settle for the ordinary."
Jim Rohn

"There is only one way to avoid criticism:
Do nothing, say nothing, and be nothing."
Aristotle

"If you don't build your dream, someone else will hire you
to help them build theirs."
Dhirubhai Ambani

"Always go with your passions. Never ask yourself if it's realistic or not."
Deepak Chopra

"The most important thing to remember is this: to be ready at any moment
to give up what you are for what you might become."
W. E. B. Du Bois

"Leap and the net will appear."
Zen saying

"Often the difference between a successful man and a failure is not one's better
abilities or ideas, but the courage that one has to bet on his ideas,
to take a calculated risk, and to act."
Maxwell Maltz

"I've missed more than 9000 shots in my career. I've lost almost 300 games.
Twenty-six times I've been trusted to take the game-winning shot and missed.
I've failed over and over and over again in my life.
And that is why I succeed."
Michael Jordan

"When you take risks you learn that there will be times when you succeed and
there will be times when you fail, and both are equally important."
Ellen DeGeneres

"The best time to plant a tree was twenty years ago.
The second best time is now."
Chinese Proverb

"Don't worry about failures,
worry about the chances you miss when you don't even try."
Jack Canfield

"Twenty years from now you will be more disappointed by the things that you
didn't do than by the ones you did do, so throw off the bowlines, sail away from
safe harbor, catch the trade winds in your sails. Explore, dream, discover."
H. Jackson Brown

"Everything you've ever wanted is on the other side of fear."
George Addair

"Risk more than others think is safe.
Care more than others think is wise.
Dream more than others think is practical.
Expect more than others think is possible."
Cadet maxim

"Screw it, Let's do it!"
Richard Branson

"The ABCs of success: You will **Achieve**, when you **Believe**
and **Conceive** of a new future."
Paul Finck

MY FIRST MAVERICK MOMENTS

Paul Finck

*"Whenever you find yourself on the side of the majority,
it is time to pause and reflect."*
—Mark Twain

"Maverick," they said. "That is you."

It was as if I was hearing the word *maverick* for the first time.

Maverick is defined as "someone who refuses to play by the rules. He or she isn't scared to cross the line of conformity." As a matter of fact, Mavericks tend to write their own rule book.

I stated to think back to different periods of my life. I began to reflect on the decisions I had made. I realized that *"I am Maverick"* . . . and have been for a very long time. Even more profound for me was the realization that the more I was a nonconformist, the more I acted unconventionally, the more successful I became.

I have achieved a lifelong career of amazing experiences. I have developed a varied and diverse resume. I have created a freedom in my life and my career that few can even imagine. I have achieved a level of "Financial Power" that has enabled me to enjoy life to its fullest.

Some of the most profound Maverick moments were centered on my firsts—the first time accomplishing, doing, experiencing something . . . how it shaped and moved me over the years. I showed up as a Maverick, created results, and shifted along the way with every turn.

My First JOB

I graduated from college with a psychology degree and went straight into medical sales. The company I choose to work for offered me a decent salary with a slight commission override. Most people would have been satisfied with that—but not the Maverick in me.

After seven weeks—just long enough for me to move into an apartment and paint it—I quit! Imagine: College graduate quits his first paying job after seven weeks. Mom and Dad must have been so proud. I quit to go work for the competition who offered a straight commission *only*. What was I thinking?

I was thinking, *I want to be motivated, inspired, and challenged with my position—or BUST!* It was a *Maverick move.* It was unconventional and unnerving to my family. So what happened? I more than doubled my original income that year, and I enrolled one of my best friends to join me in the journey. Now I was cooking!

I learned some key lessons early on. I learned about myself, which is one of the greatest lessons you can ever learn. I learned that I love a challenge, and that I am inspired by greater expectations of myself. I also learned to follow my gut. (I was to learn later in life that this is one of the keys to success, which Napoleon Hill called "the sixth sense" in his book *Think and Grow Rich*).

Let's fast-forward to one year later. It is now 1987. I am an "experienced" twenty-two-year-old. The firm I am working for is being closed down for "billing infractions" with Medicare and Medicaid. Suddenly I am without a job. The normal reaction would be to go find another job. The *Maverick reaction*: Take note of the opportunity and get into action.

My First Company

I observed that not only was I out of a job, so were dozens of other quality salespeople in my local region. I got busy creating a new company, a sales organization for home care products . . . one of a kind in that day. I negotiated large commissions for my team with several small local companies that had no sales force. They would act as our fulfillment house. With that done, I convinced seven of the top reps in the area to represent us. Within two weeks, with the help of a partner, we were up and running with a new company, new marketing material, new structure, and new responsibilities. What a Maverick move!

I realized, at that moment, a principle I teach to my coaching students and upper level mastermind students to this day: *There is a solution to every challenge.*

I also acknowledged that I had two choices: lead or follow. Most of us are faced with that choice regularly in our lives. Where your life takes you will often be determined by which path you take—lead or follow. As with everything, it is your choice, and it was mine at the time. I chose to *lead*.

I continued engaging in different ventures and opportunities over the years, and then I got introduced to real estate in 2003. Wow—was I excited! I read every book. I listened to every CD. I went to all the seminars. I analyzed property after property, calling on realtors and brokers, looking up in the newspapers (yes, this was before everything was listed on the internet) for anything that looked like it might fit my criteria. In my first thirty days, I analyzed over one hundred properties to find THE ONE—and I found it!

Only it didn't show up the way I thought it would.

My First Investment Property

I knew I wanted a multi-unit property that cash-flowed. I thought I would end up buying a three- or four-family house. Instead I got introduced to a commercial strip mall. You read that right—a strip mall! Who would have figured? I would be stepping up big time.

Facing my fears, I did it anyway. And that one property led to another, and another, which then led to other opportunities. You see, that one property did more for me than just give me a good ROI. It gave me the confidence to "Go Big or Go Home." For instance, when I signed the papers in the real estate broker's office, even though my anxiety was so great that I thought I was going to vomit right on his mahogany table, I was able to face my fears and create a better life in the process.

One day I got introduced to a gentleman at a networking event. I was positioned as a peer, although at the time I felt like I was the young pup still wet behind the ears. In the introduction, it was suggested to this gentlemen that I would be a great addition for the multi-authored book he was producing. My first internal instinct? *Run.* My first external response: Say YES!

My First Book

As I heard myself agree, I heard the response come back to me: "Sounds great; however, we need your chapter in to us in three days. Can you get it done?" What would you say? Would the prospect of writing your first book cause you to get paralyzed with fear? For me it was motivating. I sat down, and in three days I wrote a full chapter. I remember the publisher checking in with me a couple times a day to confirm I was going to make the deadline. Within the month the book was launched, and I became a best-selling author for the first time.

Through all of this, I experienced first-hand the power of singularity of focus and setting clear deadlines (another Maverick lesson which has served me well over the years). I stepped up, did a first, and proved once again that the magnitude of my quality of life comes from my *Maverick behavior.*

I had created some success in real estate and was doing some coaching and training. I was still working through some of my own anxiety about being on stage when I was asked to speak. The conference organizers wanted me to do a complete two-day program all on my own. I would be the headliner and carry the show. By this point, I had become used to saying yes to whatever came up. So when the opportunity arrived, I said yes right away . . . and then felt shocked inside for the rest of the night.

Now here was the fun part—days turned into weeks, weeks turned into months, and I still had heard no official word as to when this seminar was to take place. Then one day, I got a call from an assistant asking if I needed anything, and if I was ready. "Ready? Ready for what?" She proceeded to inform me the date and location had been set; the advertising had gone out; I was scheduled to speak in five weeks.

My First Speaking Gig

Oh boy—there was no way I was ready. The first time on my own, speaking for two full days; it was too much to prepare for . . . "I cannot do this!" is what I heard screaming in my head. I was so scared that I spent the next three weeks thinking about all the ways I could get out of doing it. Let me tell you, some crazy things can cross your mind when you are that scared. Finally, though, I realized there was no way to avoid the situation, so it was time to get ready for it. But how?

I spent the remaining two weeks before the event preparing for the big day by . . . *visualizing* the event. I did not have the time to prepare what I would say, memorize it, practice it, videotape my practice, replay my video, and make adjustments—all of which would have been really helpful. The only thing I could do with the time I had left was to visualize. I visualized the room, the people, the MC announcing my name, the crowd giving me a standing ovation as I took the stage. I visualized every segment, the tempo and the rhythm of the words, segment by segment. Day one visualized. Day two visualized. I did this over and over again. I swear my wife thought I was goofing off. I would lay on the couch, close my eyes, and go through every part of the seminar.

Here is the most amazing part of the story: When the day came, I looked into the room, I saw the audience, I heard the MC announcing my name, I ran up on stage, and the audience gave me a standing ovation before I even opened my mouth—just like I had visualized! The rest of the seminar went off beautifully. Big *Maverick moment*! I learned the power of positive thinking and visualization. Now I fully understand the concept—what you believe is true! Believe always.

As a best-selling author, international key note speaker, trainer, business consultant, and coach to entrepreneurs and real estate investors all over the world, and known as the The Maverick Millionaire®, I have learned the formula for success: deep desire, great support, quality education, and *massive action.*

In this journey, I have gone on to do millions of dollars in real estate, sold millions of dollars in informational products and services, and coached thousands of people around the world. I am passionate about coaching others to build their dream life by teaching them to "Do It Different." My decision so many years ago to take a different path in turn has created an abundant life.

Be a Maverick Do It Different™

Paul Finck is the Maverick Millionaire. *He brings to the table a vast array of skill sets, including thirty years of sales, marketing, and entrepreneurial experience. He has consulted and trained a great many industries, including the medical, dental, real estate, financial, retail, information marketing, direct sales, multilevel marketing, and speakers/coaches/trainers. He is a former mortgage broker, real estate agent, and real estate investor.*

Starting with a desire to be great, Paul learned from several of the biggest names out there and Dared to be Different—*he dared to be a Maverick. His successes include moving multimillions of dollars in real estate and over $30 million in informational products. With his primary focus on multiple streams of income, he has built up several businesses in information marketing, network marketing, and real estate investing. He now speaks and coaches internationally, teaching others how they can create this success in their own lives while they* Do It Different *and* Be a Maverick!

Paul is well known for his success and his awesome family. He and his wife, Deborah, have appeared with their three sets of twins on Good Morning America, CNN, CNN Live, The Jane Pauley Show, The Montel Williams Show, *and local Channel 8 and Channel 11 news. He has been featured in* Parents Magazine *and most local newspapers in his home state of Connecticut. All of them agree that any time spent with Paul Finck will Dare You to Be Different, Dare You to Be Great, and Dare You to Be a Maverick.*

When you want direct answers to the tough challenges in order to get the results you are asking for in your life, Paul Finck is the one you want! With more than thirty years as an entrepreneur, he knows what it takes to build a business with sustainable success. As a husband and father of three sets of twins, he knows how to keep it in balance and perspective. His nontraditional methods have brought success not only to him personally, but to individuals and companies all over the world on finding unconventional answers to everyday challenges.

Paul Finck currently offers coaches entrepreneurs and small-to-midsize companies on how to double their results in private and group coaching sessions, and he appears on stages around the world speaking on using unconventional methods to build new businesses, create motivation, eliminate fear, and generate sales. He also trains on networking, negotiations, time management, real estate investing, living the life of your dreams, and quantum-leaping your success. He is available for public, private, and corporate speaking engagements, workshops, and seminars on a wide variety of topics incorporating his Maverick Difference *philosophy.*

TheMaverickDifference.com

THE BIG "BREAK":
WHAT YOU THINK, YOU GET

Keith Meals

It was few years ago and my fiancé, her daughter, and I were headed to an ice-skating party. As we drove past the local hospital, I remember thinking it had been a long time since I had been there.

About two hours later, as I stepped on the ice for the first time in years, I was confident. I used to ice skate a couple times a month growing up in western Pennsylvania. I started to make my first lap around the rink. As I rounded the far end of the rink picking up speed, my right skate caught the back of my other skate while crossing over. Down I went! My hands went down to catch myself . . . and POP! I heard it and felt it. I knew immediately my wrist was broken. Guess where we headed immediately? I got to visit the very place I had thought about earlier. Not exactly the big break I was looking for in my life.

There was another POP! This one occurred in my head when I realized just how important lessons I had been learning during the previous few years actually were and caused what I refer to as my Big Break. My journey to the success I have created with multiple businesses in real estate, construction, and coaching have all started with the thoughts that go through my mind. This was one lesson I repeatedly heard, but until this point, I had never realized how true it was. It was truly THE eye opener for my life to this point.

If you have never heard about the power of your thoughts, think of the title of the famous book by Napoleon Hill, *Think and Grow Rich*. In this book, Hill talks about the power of creating wealth by thinking. What I have learned through him and multiple other mentors is success starts with just an idea in your head. When you think of an idea, it puts the message out to the Universe you are looking for resources and ways to accomplish the idea. The unique part about this is that it allows for both awesome opportunities and incredible challenges, depending on what is in your mind.

Think about it for a moment. You are headed to work. You catch all the green lights on your drive. They are playing all your favorite songs. The coffee stop went smoothly, and you could swear the barista was flirting with you. Everything seems to be going your way. What kind of rest of the day do you have? Typically, it's a great day after you experience this kind of start to it.

The other side is that you wake up late. You go outside to find that your car battery is dead because you left the lights on. It takes forty-five minutes for AAA to get there to jump-start your battery. You spill coffee on your shirt as you are turning into the office parking lot. What kind of the rest of the day do you have? Typically, it's a challenging day after this kind of beginning.

Why do these two days turn out the way they do? Some will say circumstance. I say choice. **It all comes back to the same principle: You get exactly what you think about in your mind.**

Every time I have needed to create more sales in one of my businesses, I put my mind to work on creating or identifying opportunities. Each time I do this, almost amazingly these opportunities show up in my life.

One example which comes to mind from a few years ago was when my construction and remodeling company was coming into a slower period of time around the holidays. I started thinking of a list of people I could reach out to about projects they had looked at doing at various points over the year. Before I was done with the list, I received a phone call from one of them and a text message from another about my team's availability to get started on their jobs right away.

Now, this is a theme that constantly appears in my life. I think of an idea, an action, or an opportunity, and the next thing I see happen is that the resources show up, people reach out to me, and emails or texts or phone calls come in—all without me ever having done more than think about an idea or action. At times I have gone so far as to tell one of my mentors, "It's almost as though I can just dream it up—and it happens."

This principle works both ways in creating both positive and negative results, as you see from the previous examples. I have learned this lesson very well. This is where control over your thoughts becomes critical. With the Universe delivering whatever you are asking for—good or bad—the onus is on you to choose your thoughts wisely. It's the old adage: "What you focus on expands."

This is why everything seems to come up roses for those who are positive in their outlook, thoughts, and actions, while the exact opposite is true for the negative Nellies (no offense to any Nellies out there).

The way I have really focused this energy is by constantly questioning the thoughts in my head. **I constantly ask myself the question: "Does this thought serve you?"**

When it does, I continue with it. When the answer is no, I change or reframe what I am thinking to make it a serving thought. I know, it seems really simple . . . and it is once you have practiced it. The challenge for most people is doing this consistently.

Are you willing to put in the kind of effort required to change your thoughts? If you're still on the fence, know that this works in all areas of your life.

When I was figuring out the exact woman I wanted to start dating after my divorce, I sat down and wrote out a detailed description, down to body type, eye color, sense of humor, intelligence, and so on. Once I completed this activity, without even putting it out there for anyone else to see, this exact woman appeared in my life—my fiancé, Alice.

You may be saying, "This all sounds great for you, Keith. **How am I supposed to tap into this in my life?**" Great question. **First, I would encourage you to constantly read nonfiction books.** Read about personal development, historical figures, and companies with successful cultures. It's part of what I do on a daily basis.

Second, I would advise you to attend events and workshops these same types of people attend. Remember, you are the average of the five people you spend the most time with in your life. Are your current Fab Five the right ones?

One event where you can really jump-start this process is hosted by my one of my mentors multiple times each year in various locations around the US. And since you've read to this point, I have a great gift for you to step forward into this new reality. Just go to **successmavbonus.com and grab your FREE ticket** to this event as my gift to you. You'll only have to take care of the seat deposit, which will be refunded in its entirety once you attend the event. I look forward to seeing you there!

KEITH MEALS is an international coach and trainer, author, real estate investor, and entrepreneur. He loves helping others reach their potential with his results-focused coaching style. As a challenge solver, he sees opportunities where others only see issues. Since 2008 this approach has helped his students explode their businesses and their lives.

Keith has been in the construction industry in Florida since 2002. Keith's innovative ideas and responses have created an entirely new niche in the construction field with his maintenance reminder service for homeowners. This service has formed a strong foundation to help his business, On Time Home Reminders, LLC, retain clients for years as he helps them maintain the quality, functionality, and value of their home—which is most people's largest investment. He helps homeowners create their dream home with his new home construction and remodeling divisions.

Keith, his beautiful fiancé, Alice, his awesome stepdaughter, Paige, and his puppy-son, Jude (a retired AKC and UKC champion Dalmatian) live just outside beautiful Orlando, Florida.

Keith is available for coaching and consulting on your business, your home renovation/build, and creating multiple streams of income in your life. He can be reached at keith@ontimehomereminders.com.

www.ontimehomereminders.com

THE POWER OF PASSION

Mark Yuzuik

I recently watched a video on YouTube featuring various people giving their definition of passion. Here are some of the responses:

- "Passion is a living, breathing thing that keeps us interested in life and wanting to know more."
- "Passion is when you are so lost in what you are doing that time doesn't matter."
- "We all have warm embers burning inside us. Passion is when those embers start to blaze."
- "Passion adds that emotional level of response to what you do."
- "Passion is being completely alive and authentic and being able to pass that feeling on to others."

Consider these words: *workaholic! electrifying! magnetic! charismatic! enthusiastic!* All of these words have been used to describe someone who is passionate.

An accountant, for example, who works until midnight might be considered a "workaholic." A motivational speaker who gets his audience on their feet might be considered "electrifying." A salesperson with customers waiting in line might be considered "magnetic." Someone who understands how to influence and inspire people with words might be considered "charismatic."

As a speaker, people often say that they really appreciate my passion. But what do they really mean? Think about a recent speaker you've heard, enjoyed, and were inspired by. Did this individual seem to ignite the room when he or she entered? Did you wonder where this person got such boundless, endless energy? Did you wish that you had one-tenth of that energy or passion? Did you feel a little slighted or even cheated when you began comparing your passion to his or hers?

This person not only demonstrated passion—they probably also connected their passion to their purpose and their message, even igniting the passion in you when they spoke. The end result was improved performance.

To live without passion suggests that life is basically void of emotion, an empty vessel, a person merely existing, moving from one meaningless action to another and never achieving the next great step. Passion is the critical ingredient for unleashing purpose and performance. All three are necessary to achieve the dreams or results you desire for your business, your family, your relationships, your community, and yourself.

Passion is not just floating around in the atmosphere waiting to smack you upside the head one day. By taking an active approach, you can develop your passionate interests proactively and eventually find your real passion.

If you want to find and ignite the passion in your life, start by being willing to allow passion into your life.

Living with passion demands energy, commitment, and playing at a 100 percent level. That isn't always comfortable, but the rewards for allowing yourself to be passionate about something near and dear to your heart are beyond measure. The rewards for expressing your passion in all you do far outweigh the pain of staying in your comfort zone.

Think about this statement: We will all endure one of two pains in life—the pain of discipline or the pain of regret. The pain of discipline weighs ounces, while the pain of regret weighs tons.

Nine Keys to Living with Passion

1. Imagine yourself being passionate. Whether it's a particular subject you want to develop or life itself, imagine your new, passionate self. What's different? Do you smile more? Are you happier? Do you greet others with more enthusiasm? How does the "passionate you" look and feel to you?

2. Play the "what if?" game with yourself. Once you've become knowledgeable and have acquired a certain level of skill, challenge the currently accepted theories in that area. New inventions are created this way.

3. Allow yourself to connect with the things that are most important to you. What matters most to you in the world? What causes are you willing to take a stand for? What are you willing to fight for? What angers you most in the world? What is it that, when you talk about it to others, makes your voice strengthen with emotion and passion? Use your imagination. Think! Feel! Believe! Take action!

4. Identify role models. If you can, learn something about them and their passions. Specifically learn about how their passions were developed. I know a man who is a multibillionaire. At age fourteen, he dropped out of school and joined a street gang. He was homeless for a number of years and ate out of dumpsters. A few years ago, he was ranked the twenty-fourth richest person in America. To me, that's inspiring. It tells me that anybody can do anything they want when they find their passion and act on it.

5. Take inventory. By now you've probably discovered that most people are not born with their passion. Rather, it develops over time out of an interest.

6. Nurture and develop your passions. Nurture the existing interests you identify, or develop new ones. This step may need to be repeated multiple times until you develop a true passion.

7. Take action. Passion isn't just about being interested in something. Passion is about action. Your passion compels you! Sitting back and waiting isn't an option.

8. Make sure that you don't derail that passion with limitations. Sometimes an issue you feel passionate about seems too big. You wonder, "What can I do? I'm only one person. How can I learn and accomplish everything there is to do?"

9. Learn to let go of old habits by becoming self-observant. Letting go of outdated habits requires an act of self-observation. Self-observation is different from self-awareness. You can be "aware" that you are feeling fearful or depressed or that your attitude stinks, but self-observation takes it to another level. You can actually observe yourself feeling a certain way. Once you know and feel the passion that fuels you, become observant of your actions and which ones are not fueling your passion. Are your actions moving you toward what you want or away from it? If you let your fears direct your business or your life instead of your passion, either way you will always end up with more of the same.

Feed the feelings that fuel your passion; give yourself permission to go after what you want most. Give yourself permission to be successful. Give yourself permission to be financially independent. Give yourself permission to feel good about your direction in life. The time will be right for you to accomplish something great only when you are passionately drawn to it.

So set your course. What do you want to accomplish? Why do you do what you do? How do you want your life to be? If you could live your life on your own terms—and you can—what would that look like to you? If you could do anything you wanted professionally, what would it be? What would be your ideal income or net worth? Make sure that you have a burning desire, an internal heat hot enough to move you past just wishful thinking. Let your dream consume you and drive you to action.

Consider these three words: *passion, performance*, and *purpose*. Now imagine someone standing with outstretched arms and open hands, one hand holding the word passion and the other holding the word *purpose*.

What I would like you to consider is that passion is the present moment where others, as well as you, see your emotions. Purpose is the future, your true direction, that which you constantly strive toward in order to reach your goal. Performance is the individual with the outstretched hands. Performance is the collection of all past experiences and current actions where you continually apply knowledge as you hold your passion and purpose. You can look in the eyes of any individual and know whether they have passion and purpose or not. How about you? What is your passion? What is your purpose?

I hope you'll challenge yourself to live with passion and take a few chances so that you can celebrate your life and your calling. Be absolutely, positively, passionate—because passion creates a life worth living!

MARK YUZUIK is most widely known as a stage hypnotist performing all over the country. However, there is much more to him than most of his fans realize. Mark has been wowing audiences with his hypnotic stage shows since 1991. He has performed in over ten thousand events for over five million people all over the world, from Australia, Europe, South America to Canada.

Mark's success at state fairs, corporate events for PDS, Robin Robins, real estate companies, Toshiba, Petco, South West Container, Mercedes, Toyota, and many more. Mark has the ability to positively and powerfully impact the quality of life for everyone involved.

Mark Yuzuik is a true picture of what is possible when someone truly commits themselves to something bigger than themselves. Raised in a family where love was abundant, Mark grew up with his thirst for creating wealth only exceeded by his passion for helping other people. Mark also conducts multiday seminars called Total Transformation with Hypnosis. Mark surrounds himself with people who are willing to hold him accountable to the standards he needs to live by in order to maximize his talents. He teaches that simply having the knowledge is not enough. Mark's love of people and his passion for making a difference shine through his words and his presence on stage.

www.markyuzuik.com

THREE SECRETS TO ALIGN YOUR MIND TO WIN

Matt Brauning

Some people seem to have all the luck. They try their hand at a new business venture, a relationship, or new skill, and it works, while some of us keep swinging at the same ball but never seem to hit it out of the park.

Those "out of the park hitters" seem to share certain mental patterns that set them up for success. Try these secrets on for size so you can begin to achieve the same results.

Get Uncomfortable

Experts say that it takes twenty-one days to change a habit. Or was it seven days? Thirty days? I've heard many stories about how difficult it is to change. The reality? Change always happens in an instant—the trick is predicting the instant . . .

Imagine that you have been driving to work using the same route, day in and day out, for thirty years. Then one day someone shows you a shortcut. How long would it take for you to change and take the shortcut? Thirty days? Would you change one street at a time, since you've followed that pattern for so long?

Of course not. Change happens in an instant, but we need to find the shortcut. Often that shortcut initially will feel uncomfortable. It's a road you've never been down before.

I had been going to our church for about a year, and one day our pastor asked if I would preach a message on a Sunday morning about a month out. I was floored! I had just been sharing with him something I believed God was showing me, but I never imagined myself speaking to the whole church!

Looking back on that day, I had a choice. Would I step up and do something I didn't feel ready for at all, or would I stay with what I knew and pass on the opportunity? I wasn't ready, but I said, "Of course, I would love to."

Sunday morning came, and I was as prepared as I could be. I had my notes, my Bible, and my nerves, all ready to go. There are defining moments in our life when we must choose to step up or step back.

Sometimes the very best new opportunities don't feel great a first, but they end up proving to be very fruitful. The secret is to look for something uncomfortable, then follow it. It can actually be a sign that it's a change you are looking for.

Since that day, I have preached many times. I look back at my life now and wonder what it would be like if I had said no that day.

Get uncomfortable and say yes.

Ask Questions

It's shocking how much the human brain can learn—and even more shocking that many people think they've arrived at a full wealth of knowledge.

The human brain has 1010 to the 11th possible neurological connections. That's the number ten with ten zeros . . . written eleven times! That number is more than the estimated grains of sand on the earth and more than the stars in the known universe!

The reality is that we are truly limitless as humans. How could we ever "arrive" at knowing everything? It's pretty silly when you stop to think about it.

So how do we reverse the know-it-all trap? Remember a time in your life when you had more questions than answers? For me, it was when I was about five years old.

I knew just enough to realize that there was a lot more to know. My number one question was always "why." Why is the sky blue? Why do fish swim in the water? Why are Doritos shaped like triangles?

When we return to a time when we didn't have all the answers, we can begin to solve our problems very fast. We don't need better quality answers; we need to ask a better quality question.

I consulted with a well-known Fortune 500 company a few years ago regarding customer engagement. I asked them for the top ten questions they had been asking themselves while attempting to turn around the dropping engagement scores.

The top two questions were: "Why are our customers dissatisfied?" and "Who are they buying from instead?"

In our own lives, we ask questions like these all the time. "Why can't I find a decent relationship?" or "Why can't I stick with a diet for more than a couple of days?"

If you ask a bad question, you will get a bad answer. But if you ask a powerful question, you'll get a powerful answer! Our outcomes are determined by the type of questions we ask.

Try asking questions that assume a resourceful answer:

"How can we find the very thing our customers truly desire?"

"How can we deliver the best possible experience for them?"

"How do we grow to become the leader in our industry, and make a massive positive impact on our community?"

When we begin to realize that we don't need to have all the answers—we just need better questions, that's where success begins.

Maintain a Single Focus

To focus or not to focus: That is the question. On one hand, if we focus intently on one goal, that seems to be the way of progress. On the other, some of the greatest success stories in the last one hundred years are about people with ADD or dyslexia—people who think about dozens of ideas at once!

The truth is that either way works. But when I say a single focus, what I actually mean is a single focus of direction. Our goals and actions cannot take us in opposite directions.

A young businessman came to one of my workshops saying he wanted to succeed so badly, but kept falling short of his goals. I took him through a simple process, first asking, "What's important about succeeding in business?" His top four answers were:

1. Making money
2. Having freedom
3. Giving back
4. Doing what I'm passionate about

This short list would turn out to be his list of subconscious values, those things that were most important to him.

Our goals cannot take us in opposite directions. If this man's number one value, or goal, was making money, there were certain actions he would need to take. He would need to work on marketing, make sales calls, work with clients, have team meetings, and so on.

Those types of actions would move him closer to his goal of success. The conflict showed up when we looked at his next value: having freedom.

If having freedom was important, perhaps he would want to make his own schedule. He might want to have mornings free to sleep in, or take Tuesdays off to go ski—whatever freedom meant to him.

My advice was simple. Each day he could either take actions that lead him closer to success or take actions that lead him closer to freedom. He can't have both at the same time.

As you think about your own values and goals, consider which one is the most important and move in that direction. Think, *If I could only have one, which one would I choose?*

You can have more than one, but there is always a subconscious hierarchy of these values. If you don't recognize this, you may find yourself in deep conflict. One day you might work very hard, and then feel trapped because you don't take enough time off. But when you do take time off, you realize that sales have decreased.

Consider picking one as your top value, and make the others future goals. Tell yourself, "I may not have a ton of freedom right now, but that's OK because I am building success right now. I have a goal of freedom in the future, and that's worth working toward!"

MATT BRAUNING speaks extensively and runs seminars all over the world training coaches, speakers, and entrepreneurs how to grow their businesses while making a massive impact with their work. Matt captivates all types of audiences with an honest, hilarious, and exciting look into how our lives really work. He founded Evolution in 2006 as a way to make an impact in the world through personal development and education.

Matt received training from Anthony Robbins as part of his exclusive Platinum Partnership group and was filmed in the hit movie The Journey with Brian Tracy and Bob Proctor. He now consults with Fortune 100 companies, and his client list includes US Bank, The YMCA, John McAfee of McAfee Antivirus, Project Management Institute (PMI), and New York Life, among others. He is also the pastor of a local church.

As an entrepreneur, best-selling author, and Master Trainer of NLP, Matt is a leader in the field of business development and human potential. He is an avid rock climber and motorcyclist. He lives in Orange County with his amazing wife, Lola, and awesome son, Valiant.

How to Sell Before You Finish Your Rehab

Reggie Brooks

The average abandoned and distressed property investor approaches the rehab and resale process the same way:

1. They acquire a property.
2. They rehab the property.
3. They plant a "For Sale" sign in the front yard.
4. They sell the property.
5. They smile triumphantly at a job well done.

If you're following this model, you are quite possibly succeeding in real estate. But did you know that by shaking up the order in which you approach your rehab projects, you can dramatically increase the number of rehab projects you can complete in a year—and at the same time reach your goal of financial independence much more quickly?

While you can't do much about steps 1, 2, and 5, steps 3 and 4 can be reversed, meaning that over the course of an investing career you could earn millions more than an investor who follows the traditional model. It's easier than you think.

The first thing you'll want to do is plant a large "For Sale" sign in the front yard. While you want to ensure that your telephone number is on the sign, you can actually modify your sign and generate calls from potentially interested buyers and sellers. Here's an example of language you could place on your sign that could potentially get your phone ringing off the hook:

FOR SALE
3BR 2BA Currently Being Renovated
Call Now and You Can Pick Paint Colors, Carpet Styles, and More
Call Now! Priced to Sell
555-1234

Before beginning the inside work, tidy up the outside of the property. While you may think that the interior of the property is the most important part of a rehab project, I'm here to tell you that what happens on the outside can create instant curb appeal and generate tremendous interest.

By creating curb appeal and generating interest, you can more quickly sell the property. Here's a simple, easy-to-follow blueprint for success:

Clean up the exterior and make it look as good as possible. What you do on the outside need not be extensive—or expensive. After placing a "For Sale" sign in the front yard, decide what simple landscaping measures will maximize the property's curb appeal.

You'd be amazed by how much curb appeal a property can gain by simply cleaning up the front yard, adding some wood chips around the trees, and planting a few colorful bushes or shrubs in the front and on both sides of the house.

In addition, don't ignore the appearance of the house itself. If it has shutters, simply replacing them can instantly double a property's appeal—and can get people interested in seeing what changes you have in mind for the interior.

Tidy up the exterior of the house by touching up the paint on the wood trim and doing other little things to give the house a fresh, welcoming look.

There's an added benefit to doing things in this order: It is actually possible to sell the property before completing the renovations.

Your "For Sale" sign combined with the interest-generating landscaping and other improvements will likely generate some calls from interested parties. When they call, you can offer to show the property to them as it is now. By giving them the opportunity to possibly pick out the color of carpet, paint, and so on, you will generate tremendous interest, because the average home buyer either makes minor changes immediately after buying a house or makes a mental note to change certain things not long after buying it.

A Winning Strategy

Here's where this strategy can pay huge dividends. If a potential buyer gets to decide what color they want the carpet and paint to be, they will automatically have more interest in buying than they would if the renovations have already been made.

If they like what they see, you can place the house under contract and collect an earnest money deposit, which you could use to help pay for renovations.

There's another possible way of selling before completing your rehab: Some buyers will ask if you would be willing to sell at a discount if they made the repairs themselves. This is a great idea that will allow you to more quickly cash out of the property that you're getting ready to rehab.

Many buyers are handy around the house and are willing to put some sweat equity into a property, particularly if they think that they could save money.

While you won't be able to sell every property you buy before completing your renovation work, it does happen fairly regularly. This will allow cash to flow more quickly into your bank account—and allow you to more quickly move on to your next profitable investment.

If you like, you can continue waiting until your renovations have been completed before selling the property, but by following my model, you'll be able to buy more properties.

Think Long Term

Using this model, over the course of a twenty- or thirty-year real estate investing career, you could possibly buy and sell several more properties per year than you would otherwise.

Thinking outside the box and defying expected norms is just one way you can blast into increased real estate profitability.

Another way is by continuing to learn additional real estate tips and tricks. This is how you can gain an edge on the competition.

By following the tips I've shared with you, you can quickly turn an ordinary investing career into a special one that makes you rich beyond your wildest dreams.

REGGIE BROOKS has achieved what many people consider to be impossible. He went from making $36,000 per year at the local telephone company to making over $40,000 per month in his real estate business. Starting out with very little money, Reggie began his investment career in 1986. After taking several real estate investment courses, he began investing in rental properties in Los Angeles. By educating himself about the hidden opportunities in real estate and making well-placed investments, he has become a multimillionaire.

Reggie is an international speaker and lecturer, author, and active real estate investor. Reggie has spoken on programs with such notables as Donald Trump, Magic Johnson, Suze Orman, Anthony Robbins, George Foreman, Rudy Giuliani, Dr. Albert Lowry, Alan Greenspan, David Bach, and Russell Simmons.

Over the years, he has developed his Success Systems that consistently turn marginal $15,000 to $20,000 real estate deals into $50,000 to $75,000 deals. Reggie teaches his *system all over America. "It's very simple when you take the time to learn how," Reggie says. His students say that the combination of his insightful knowledge with a sheer joy for teaching makes the learning process pleasurable.*

Reggie has earned the respect of the real estate investment community as well as the seminar community because of his many investment accomplishments and his ability to teach them in a seminar or classroom setting. Of his many successful students, Reggie is most proud of his two kids, Keith and Arlett. Through his mentoring they have both become successful, full-time millionaire real estate investors.

www.reggiebrooks.com

Honor. Sanctitude. Resilience.

Kelly Carter

The lights are dimmed. I breathe deeply and relax as I sit with my spine erect on my chair. I close my eyes as one of my dearest mentors delivers me through a guided meditation. I picture a workshop of my own design, a sacred space, so-to-speak, where I am inspired to create and invent. Here, I am to discover my principles, the cornerstones by which I live my life. I ask myself repeatedly, "What are my principles?" Almost instantly, the word honor *comes to mind. To me, it encompasses acceptance, respect, responsibility, integrity, and reverence. It is something I can take pride in and is a logical choice on many levels.*

I continue asking. Then, what seems like out of nowhere comes the word sanctitude. *This is not an everyday word, to say the least, and I feel oddly puzzled and surprised. Again I ask, "What are my principles?" Again a third word materializes, and again I wonder from where it has come, knowing full well that my mind somehow plucked it from the ether:* resilience.

While not a full-on wordsmith, words do fascinate me, and I often find myself looking up definitions and etymologies of words to be sure I understand their meanings. These last two words sparked my curiosity. In my research, I found *sanctitude* to mean "sacredness, deep respect, and reverence." I interpret it as a reminder to see the divinity in everything. *Resilience* simply means "the power to rebound or recover readily." It reminds me of a Japanese proverb I love: "Fall down seven times, get up eight," to which I like to add "and learn how to stop falling so often."

These three words are now my gift to myself. They are my principles; they are what keep me going even when it "seems" like nothing else may be going my way—for instance when my world did a 180 back in June of 2012. Now, I have been involved in a multitude of personal development, consciousness, spiritual, and awareness types of training my whole life. My mother and grandmother used to take me with them to various classes and lectures as a child. On into my adulthood, my husband and I began our own journey into similar pursuits as well as many entrepreneurial endeavors. We studied with some of the best and mirrored them to create our own success. We found great joy in supporting others in doing the same, and in turn we also created a coaching and mentoring business.

Things were really good. We were traveling, flying on private jets, meeting wonderful people, and expanding our businesses and connections. I loved being able to work side by side with my life partner. We did have our challenges, both in business and in our personal lives, as life is not always that proverbial bed of roses. It was nothing insurmountable, and I was committed to having it all work out together. We were in the process of learning some new tools, and I was excited to have new ways of communicating and working together. And then one evening my husband approached me and told me he was not committed to our marriage anymore.

Others may have chosen this as a solution to the challenges we faced. In my mind, it was never an option. I had thought we were in agreement on that. I was wrong . . . and I was devastated. Everything we had was comingled: our funds, our expenses, our debts, our businesses. Now it would all unravel. We never had children. We did have two super senior dogs that ended up passing away within six months of each other during this time. Shortly thereafter, while changing clothes one night, I noticed a lump in my breast. My husband was leaving, our businesses were dismantled, my beloved pets were gone, and now I was facing a health challenge. Tests confirmed the undesired diagnosis. Two surgeries resulted to ensure the margins were clear, followed by a sequence of radiation treatments.

I could have curled up into a ball and just stopped . . . and that was not an option in alignment with my principles. Instead, I used the opportunity to take a long, hard look at myself and who I had been. I saw that I had not been not operating as the highest version I could imagine myself to be. I was only being what I could accept. I needed to raise my standards. I made up my mind to truly have that loving, committed, communicative, joyful relationship, no matter what. I had to figure out *who* I wanted to be and *how* I wanted to be—for me. Reinvention was key. I knew that I would need to be the change I wanted to see. Did I get angry sometimes? Were there tears? Heck, yeah! Yet through it all, I kept reminding myself of my commitment. When I fell off track, I would dust myself off, make a plan, and go for it again—rinse and repeat as necessary.

Throughout this process, I had thought I would somehow salvage my marriage. What ended up happening was so much more than I could imagine. I noticed how much more I liked myself; I felt comfortable in my own skin again. I saw where I had been giving my power away. Through my metamorphosis, something extraordinary happened. I met a man that actually had gone to junior high school with me. In school, he was one year ahead of me, and while we did not really know each other back then, I did remember him. When we met as adults, he was newly divorced. He also has two young boys, which is so awesome because I now get to experience what it is like having children in my life. Since the beginning, we have created nothing but joy, connection, and outstanding memories. I love creating our family and partnership together, and we choose each other every day.

Choosing my principles and living by them has given me a blank canvas to create and invent a new lease on life. I have chosen to never let any of the challenging times I have experienced define me—not the divorce, not the illness. I have reached the point where I can say I am grateful for all of it and all it has taught me. I choose who I am, and I author my life. As of this writing, I can now say that I am five years completely healthy! I have created the relationship of my dreams. I am in demand as a speaker and coach. My other businesses and partnerships are booming as well. No matter how many times I may fall down, I continue to live in honor, sanctitude, and resilience. I learn, and I will always get back up . . . every time.

 *KELLY CARTER specializes in various genres of coaching. She has coached many clients in their entrepreneurial, real estate, and marketing pursuits. In the last five years, her primary focus has become more personal-results driven: "What is it you are looking for and how can you get there?"*

At seventeen years old Kelly held a prominent position in corporate America. Despite her young age, people naturally gravitated to her space seeking answers or new directions for growth, both personally and professionally. Being a natural leader, she has combined her life experiences and continued studies to assist those she trains, teaches, coaches, or manages to achieve maximum success. Kelly truly touches the lives of all those she encounters.

Entering into the seminar world in the areas of personal development in 2006, she learned about life strategies for personal power, health, relationships, and more. Kelly then broadened her understanding by moving into hypnosis, where she has incorporated a deeper understanding of how the mind works, why people do what they do, and what causes real change. Constantly emphasizing the importance of a positive mindset, Kelly consistently inspires those she engages to achieve their desired results regardless of circumstances.

The HVAC Marketing Wheel [Reinvented]

Sam Garwood

I've been in the HVAC business for over twenty years. I started in the commercial industry as a sheet metal worker, where I got to see all the different ways we can use sheet metal—from the gold leaves at the nearby Notre Dame Golden Dome to the pipes and ducts that vent the bathrooms at the local Juvenile Center. Thanks to my uncle, Neal Garwood Sr, my dad had the opportunity to be a sheet metal worker, and eventually my dad would make the same opportunity available to me. Uncle Neal was one of the best friends and mentors a man could have ever have.

At the time I was studying about time management and Henry Ford, who is credited for revolutionizing the car industry by utilizing the assembly line. So one of the first things I did, as a beginner in the trade, was to break down the movements and tools used in certain applications so I could combine them and increase my productivity. I did very well by my calculations, because after only a year or two I was outperforming guys that had been in the industry thirty-plus years. I thought I had earned the respect of my colleagues by outproducing them in every aspect of the job. I found out a few years later that I had done the opposite; they were not interested in producing more. They were only interested in keeping things the way they were.

One of the things I noticed as a sheet metal worker was that everyone was basically doing the same things they'd always done, the same way they'd always done them. Some of the practices were as much as a century old, some of the old-timers who had trained me said. I respect tradition, and I believe we should acknowledge where we came from and how we got here. However, I do not believe we should let tradition restrict our growth. Even Uncle Neal had started a business, and from the outside it appeared that he did everything right. However, after only about five years he had to shut down his business. Why? I say it's because he was doing what everyone else was doing and simply trying to do it better.

Have you ever heard someone say, "Don't reinvent the wheel" or "Pioneering doesn't pay"? I agree with those statements to an extent. There's no need to reinvent for the sake of reinventing. However, once something has been "perfected," the only way to go beyond the known limits is to break the mold and reinvent it.

I left the commercial industry around 2000 and entered into the residential HVAC industry. I started my own HVAC business in 2002. At first I picked up extra work from companies that had more work than they could handle. Then, through word-of-mouth, people started hiring me to replace and install systems in their homes. This continued to increase as the years passed, and eventually I hired employees and bought more trucks. One of the biggest challenges I have had is keeping a steady workflow for my employees. There are a lot of factors involved, and successful HVAC companies all use traditional marketing to balance their workflow. You can tell when one of these companies is looking for more work because you will get multiple mailers, see them on TV, and hear their ads on the radio constantly.

I eventually decided to take a class that gave us everything we needed to grow and manage our HVAC business like the big companies. It was an intense course that covered all the existing systems for marketing, bookkeeping, and management. These are the systems that have been used by large HVAC businesses for decades, I was told. Following what I learned in the course, we hired a mail marketing company and made a TV commercial with a local station. However, we saw very minimal returns on our investments. Why? Remember, these systems have been used by my competitors for decades.

You can also buy into a franchise. They will give you their systems and marketing strategies once you pay a lump sum up front and give them a large percentage of your earnings. To do either one effectively, you have to increase your overhead significantly, and that means raising your prices significantly. They use marketing to create an image that makes it seem like the high prices they charge are worth it.

I decided to break the mold and explore new business models. I built my business on word-of-mouth referrals. Our customers were so happy with us that they told their friends and loved ones about us. It is not uncommon for us to have several generations of families doing business with us. The model of spending money to create a false image would be a slap in the face to our customers. Besides, in that system, even the owners and high-level management are simply doing a job. I want freedom and a real sense of contribution for myself and my employees.

To recap, successful HVAC businesses basically all do the same things. They spend a lot of money on traditional marketing and pass on that cost to the people who buy from them. They've "perfected" that system. This makes it limited, meaning that only a select few will make it, and those that do won't be much different than the others. Once something has been "perfected," the only way to go beyond the known limits is BREAK the mold and reinvent it. I've decided to do just that. And it can be done in any business.

I operate my business on the principles of integrity, quality, care, and support for both my customers and employees. Now we also are adding the principle of giving. Read on to find out how.

There are many benefits to maintaining your HVAC system. Most failures can be prevented by proper maintenance. The maintenance we provide covers safety, efficiency, and failure prevention. Today we are offering a maintenance program to everyone in our area that includes things like the filter, humidifier pad, and no overtime fees if service is needed outside of normal business hours. We are giving this away for free for one year. We plan to give away one thousand of them next year and every year after. Some of the people who will receive this gift will have never had their system maintained, and if it weren't free, they would likely never pay for it. Most of the colleagues I've shared this idea with think I'm crazy because all they see is lost revenue. I believe that any product worth buying has something worth giving away. If people do business with you and like it, they will repeat that business and tell their friends. This is grassroots marketing, and it can only be successful if the product you offer is actually worth buying.

SAMUAL GARWOOD is from the small town of Edwardsburg, Michigan, where he has been the owner and founder of a HVAC company since 2002. His company has serviced the greater Michiana area for over fifteen years. Sam's exploration in the field of personal development started in the early 90s and has led him to become a sanctioned speaker for the Global Information Network and certified as a trainer by Trainer Design Global and Gratitude Training. Sam has mentored other HVAC business owners and spent thousands of hours as a success and accountability coach. Sam is now reinventing the way marketing is done in his industry through the spirit of giving. Diagnosed with severe Crohn's disease when he was eighteen years old, Sam has taught himself to manage his disease through the power of food without ever needing surgery or any prescriptions for over fifteen years and has experienced little to no symptoms. Sam has spent countless hours studying the body, food, and health to achieve this. Therefore Sam knows what it takes to meet the challenges of balancing work and personal life.

Becoming a Marketplace Whisperer

Bridget Brady

Being an entrepreneur is hard. Like really f-ing hard. If it were easy, everyone would do it. No one really tells us this. Instead, we go to seminars in fancy hotels, and the well-spoken millionaires at the front of the room joke, laugh, and regale us with stories about hot-air balloon rides and trips around the world. They rarely tell us stories about middle-of-the-night panic attacks, their star team members leaving to work for someone else, putting rent on credit cards when cash flow is low, or simply sitting at their desk crying because "the buck" doesn't just stop here—when you are a business owner, *all* the "bucks" stop here. Sounds dismal, and yet I wouldn't trade it for a J.O.B. Not now, and likely not ever. Most of the time, the rewards outweigh the difficulties, and *all* of the time, I like to be in charge of my own life, time, and destiny. And yes, there are hot-air balloon rides, and sandy beaches, and wine-tasting in faraway destinations, so I'm certainly not suggesting that you lose hope. I am suggesting that there are several techniques and tools that will make your entrepreneurial endeavors oh-so-much easier and will help you get to your goals oh-so-much more quickly. Lucky for you, I love to share!

1. Listen to your clients, your potential clients, and the marketplace. I've been a serial entrepreneur for ten years. I have tried lots of different businesses and ways to make money outside of having a job. They were not always successful. I now own a successful online marketing agency, Amp Up My Biz. It's by far the most successful business I've ever owned; yet I fought starting this specific business for about two years.

Here's why: I'm an excellent speaker. I love speaking and training and being in front of an audience. I love to empower people and help people live a life they love. I'm also a social media expert. So I thought, *Heck let's put this chocolate in that peanut butter! I'm going to do social media training, business training, speaker and sales training. This is going to be awesome! Everyone will want to come to my trainings and be empowered to build their businesses. I will make tons of money and everyone wins!*

31

And I did those trainings (actually I still do live trainings), and people came. Not many, but some, and over and over, they'd say things like, "This is the best training I've ever been to! You are amazing! But . . . I just wish you could do all of this for me."

I would respond with, "No! It's more powerful to do it yourself. Build your own business; it will be so empowering for you!"

So for about two years I referred all that business and all those clients who wanted someone to "do it for them" to colleagues of mine. And my bank account stayed small, because I simply wasn't *listening*. I was so committed to doing it *my* way that I missed what the *marketplace* was asking from me. And then one day . . . I finally listened. Today I run a very fulfilling, very successful, full-service online marketing agency where I—yes, you guessed it—*do it for them.*

Listen to what your clients and potential clients really want. Don't get stuck in what you want to do for them. Always be congruent with your true self AND provide the products and services that your *clients* want. Become a *marketplace whisperer.* Your bank account will thank you.

2. Partner with the right people. I'm not necessarily suggesting that you get an actual partner here, but I *am* suggesting that you surround yourself, and team up with people who have complementary strengths.

I personally don't know how to build websites. The head of my web and graphic design team builds some of the most beautiful websites I've ever seen. My chocolate went well with his peanut butter; I could now offer both social media marketing *and* web and graphic design to my clients! (Apparently I like chocolate and peanut butter.) It doesn't stop there. Who do you network with, spend time with, mastermind with? There are so many people and businesses that would love to have your services! Are you out in the world, offering value and teaming up with people who can help you grow your business? Are you helping other people get what they want and need? You can create incredible, symbiotic partnerships with people that aren't necessarily official partnerships but are *strategic* partnerships that will help your business grow in ways you can't grow if you're a lone wolf trying to create business in a bubble.

3. W.I.T. I learned this from one of my first mentors, T. Harv Eker: Whatever It Takes. As an entrepreneur, I'm fairly certain this is the only way to become successful.

There are no real rules to follow when you start your own business. There is no clear path. There are guidelines to learn and helpmates you'll meet along the way, but at the end of the day, *you* are the gladiator in the arena. It is your time, your dime, and your blood, sweat, and so many tears that will make it happen. Building your success can't depend on your mood, others' opinions of you, or how much sleep you got last night. When you want something badly, when you are committed to achieving it, you find a way, create a way, borrow a way, make up a way—and do *whatever it takes* to get it.

4. Stay positive and practice gratitude. Sh*t's gonna' get hard, y'all. But guess what? Life is hard for everyone at times. Work sucks for everyone sometimes! The trick is to appreciate, embrace, and celebrate all the wonderful things you have along the way.

Another mentor and dear friend of mine, Larry Broughton, taught me the importance of keeping a daily gratitude journal. I simply sit down every morning and write down what I'm grateful for. Some days it's big things like new clients, upcoming vacations, or becoming a number-one international best-selling author. Some days, when the wheel of life just doesn't seem to be turning my way and all I see are problems crashing in all around me (and I swear this is the truth), I write what I'm still grateful for in this moment, right here, right now . . . things like the ability to walk, good vision, or a place to live. At the end of the day, it's not really how things are going for us—it's how we *feel* about how things are going for us.

Being an entrepreneur is one of the most rewarding, incredible journeys you can take! I wish you huge success, and even more than that, I wish you happiness, fulfillment, and grace in your journey.

BRIDGET BRADY is an enlightened entrepreneur, speaker, best-selling author, and social media authority. Bridget has been in the information technology industry for over twenty-five years, spending seven of those years in New York City working on Wall Street.

After working in corporate America for fifteen years, she left the "rat race" and started her own business in 2007. Her company, Amp Up My Biz, is a leader in the world of online marketing. Bridget and her team provide full-service, soup-to-nuts marketing solutions including social media marketing and training, website design and development, graphic design, and speaker and sales training. Her latest book, Jobs to Jammies! *is an Amazon number-one international best seller!*

Bridget is passionate about helping business owners grow their brands, their businesses, and their bottom lines. The Amp Up My Biz mission is simple: Help you grow your business while creating more freedom and joy for you and your team.

Bridget has helped tens of thousands of entrepreneurs create and close more business. She can help you do the same!

AmpUpMyBiz.com
Facebook.com/AmpUpMyBiz
Twitter.com/TheBridgetBrady
YouTube.com/TheBridgetBrady
LinkedIn.com/in/TheBridgetBrady
Instagram.com/TheBridgetBrady
Pinterest.com/TheBridgetBrady

Living the Laptop Lifestyle

Drew Berman

Laptops and smartphones. Layoffs and downsizing. Telecommuting and working from home. These are not just words, not just tongue-and-cheek expressions. The nine-to-five is a joke . . . it's more like the eight-to-six. Shift happens and times are a'changin'.

Risky is the new safe. Getting paid for production is the new "show up and punch a time clock." The old "we will pay you as little as we can so you don't quit, and you will work just hard enough so you don't get fired" is so 2008.

Ten thousand people a day are turning sixty-five until 2030. Baby boomers are looking for an encore career. They don't want another job. They certainly don't want to be sending out resumes. Yuck. They'd rather be playing tennis or golf or walking on a beach somewhere.

Twenty-somethings coming out of school don't want to be chained to a desk and . . . *argh* . . . pick up a telephone that is actually connected to that desk. They want a life of fun and adventure. They want to tweet and blog and post and get paid for it. They certainly don't want a boss.

We are entering into a production-based society. Jobs are being replaced by robots, and foreigners, both immigrants stateside as well as from their homeland, are getting paid pennies for what normally would be high-salaried positions. Skilled professionals are getting passed over by people half their age, at half their salary.

People are looking for solutions. They want more money, yes, but they really want more free time. Your neighbors are stressed out; your colleagues are burned out; your friends are looking for a better way.

A good job is becoming an oxymoron. I have one friend who went to Yale and is highly trained in hospital management and in running medical practices. Since I've known him, he has had two or three jobs in only seven years. It doesn't seem like he ever has enough time in the day, and he certainly doesn't seem very secure in his current gig. My cousin used to own a film and camera shop, but the internet put an end to that. He's had three or four sales jobs since then and can't seem to find himself a home. Another friend works for a top finance company and actually makes a lot of money. But after twenty years of commuting ninety minutes one way, he's kinda done with it. Every time I ask him to play golf, he's too busy.

So today I sit poolside with a beautiful view and share with you what I've learned. This morning I went for a run, and then I did a Facebook Live to share some of the life lessons I learned on that run. I called it "The Law of Attraction vs the Law of Distraction," and it was shot overlooking a beautiful marina. My head was clear after the run and my thoughts were fresh. The ideas I shared flowed freely because I am not an overweight, stressed-out, burned-out dad living for the weekend. A lot of my clients, business partners, and friends commented on that Facebook Live, and I got a ton of likes. Now, because I'm in flow, I know the likes don't mean anything. Or do they?

Because I added value to the marketplace, I know have permission to interact with the likes and with the comments. For me to get a like and not respond would be the equivalent of someone going for a high-five when you are with them in person and you not responding.

So how do I turn this into business? Well, sometimes I do, and sometimes I don't. I'll generally reach out and say something like "Thanks for liking my post on the law of attraction! What's new and good with you?"

Now, this way I have an opening to engage with folks. Whether they are friends or customers or business prospects, I have an easy opening. Then, through the art of connection, I can continue the dialogue—which sometimes leads to business.

Our business is a lifestyle business: We teach people to have a better . . . well, a better lifestyle. Imagine a triangle. Inside that triangle are the words "my perfect lifestyle." One leg of the triangle represents better health, one is more income or better wealth, and one is more free time. Which one (or ones) are you working on?

If you have two of the three, you're almost there—but something is missing. Good health and great income is nice, but without free time, it's not all that good. Good health and a ton of free time is kinda cool, but with no money, you're missing out. If you have plenty of time and a ton of money, but your health isn't good, then clearly you aren't enjoying the best lifestyle.

Here's the good news: You can have it all. You. Can. Have. It. All.

The laptop lifestyle. More time on the golf course. More time on the beach. More time to travel and pursue your dreams, goals, and hobbies. You can even have enough energy to play with you kids.

So. The business choice for millennials. The next chapter for baby boomers. The perfect opportunity for those in between. You are ready for more. You want a better life. You are ready to go from good to great.

Let's connect and dig a little deeper. For a one-on-one, no-obligation chat, reach out to me at drewaberman@gmail.com or (917) 226-6901 and mention my chapter, "The Laptop Lifestyle," from this book. For more info, check out www.drewberman.com. I look forward to assisting you with your health, wealth, and time freedom goals.

DREW BERMAN is a best-selling author, coach, trainer, mentor, and friend. He has mastered the art of merging both the online and offline world in this high tech/high tough world in which we live. Drew lives in Connecticut with his wife and two boys. He is often seen traveling, having fun, and embarking on adventures somewhere. Or you might find him at world-class masterminds, seminars, think tanks, and networking events.

Drew coaches people on the skills, habits, and mind-set required to excel in business, specifically in the profession of network marketing—the laptop lifestyle, the business of the twenty-first century, the business model that is helping people live the life they want and deserve. Some call it referral marketing; some still call it MLM. Whatever you call it, Drew is in your corner helping you win.

He has built his business with Isagenix, but through his coaching services he can help you go from hobby income to professional income in whatever company you choose. He believes that you can have it all. The perfect lifestyle has good health, lots of income, and the free time to enjoy both. If you are seeking more success in your network marketing career or looking at the profession for the first time, then you want to work with Drew. He can help you get from where you are to where you want to go.

A fun fact about Drew: In the year 2000 he rode his bicycle around the world in a thirty-five-country, 20,000-mile, 200-person, six-continent epic journey called Odyssey 2000.

LIVING THE AMERICAN DREAM

Anthony Patrick and His Team Profit in Southern California

Step into the world of Anthony Patrick, the CEO of New Harvest Ventures, LLC, based in Rancho Cucamonga, California. He's a real estate investor who loves sharing his secrets of wealth building with everyone he meets. Patrick believes education is the path toward fulfilling the American Dream. And he's doing his part to help improve the quality of his fellow men by offering his knowledge to all who seek it.

Anthony is in the business of scooping up a neglected house nobody seems to want, fixing it up, and selling it for a huge profit. What a great way to help clean up the neighborhood and build wealth at the same time! It's truly the American Dream for Patrick, his wife, Mindy, and their team partners.

Over the years Anthony and his partner, Scott Cheramie, have mastered the art of flipping houses. It certainly wasn't easy at first, and they both made costly mistakes along the way, but now they are reaping the financial rewards of staying in the game.

Anthony admits that real estate gets him excited. He says that he simply loves the adventure of the entire process of a transaction. "This business is truly my passion. I feel blessed that real estate is my life's work."

Because he went through the countless trials and errors while learning the business, Anthony says he has a lot of empathy for his students. "I've been through everything and anything you can imagine when it comes to flipping a home," he explains. And he knows the pitfalls too. Yes, he admits that he's a hand holder.

During his three-day boot camp, Anthony takes investors from around the country on a tour of his local area to see the deals he has done and those he is actively rehabbing. He works with them side by side, explaining his methods and reasons for doing things the way he does. "There's a logic to every step in flipping houses," he says. Everything is explained and everything is revealed.

Anthony often repeats himself just to ensure that everyone understands it.

He realizes that many of his students are embarking in unknown territory and he doesn't want them to make the same mistakes he made when he learned the business.

Every few months Anthony disembarks with a busload of eager students from throughout California and around the nation. Investors of all ages are anxious to learn how to rehabilitate distressed properties and make a handsome profit doing so.

Anthony's American Dream was realized through real estate. He began as a handyman, then graduated to a real estate inspector. Today, he has flipped hundreds of houses. Although he prides himself as being a "self-made man," Anthony acknowledges that he's had a lot of help to get where he is. "My beautiful wife, Mindy, is my right-hand woman. And I have a phenomenal team of brokers, real estate agents, rehabbers, contractors, and investors who have been instrumental to my success."

Anthony describes himself as a man of faith; he confides that he acknowledges the hand of God in all he does, especially in real estate. "God has guided my way throughout this journey, along with the support of my wife and our entire team," he says. But most of all, Anthony acknowledges the hand of God in all he does.

Here is Anthony's advice for his readers:

Don't wait to invest—start now. Many people don't believe they have the money to start investing, but did you know you could use some of your home's equity, or your 401(K) retirement plan from work? You can even use money from your IRA account to get started.

Although every rehab has its own strategy, the overall strategy is to provide a great product every time. You have to love what you do, and I do love flipping homes! However, it's not as glamorous as people think. The average home sells within three to six months; however, if you provide a really great product, it will usually sell within a three to four-month timeframe.

You need a system in today's market so you can get in and out as quickly as possible. Your contractors must be on the same page as you are. Remember, this business is a step-by-step process: You must know your values and understand the physical systems that will be installed in your home.

Today, as this book goes to publication, I have flipped hundreds of homes, own a real estate company, a construction company, and my team and I are even looking into building homes! This is something I love and desire—it is not a job but an adventure!

ANTHONY PATRICK is a founding member and CEO of New Harvest Ventures LLC and Real Estate Wealth Builders. He is a seasoned real estate investor, with over fifteen years of experience in several aspects of investing, including flipping homes, wholesaling, REO (real estate-owned) auctions, short sales purchases, probates, pre-foreclosures, commercial real estate, lease options, rentals and storage facilities, and more. His vast knowledge in these and other areas of real estate finance and investing have proven to be life-changing for both Anthony and his students.*

With his passion to help others build their own wealth portfolios, Anthony brings a unique perspective to the table. With his background as a handyman, home inspector, property manager, and real estate mentor, Anthony has educated thousands who want to invest and achieve success through his one-on-one training.

He has attended over one hundred seminars and has been honored to teach and speak at the same venues as other well-known professionals such as Donald Trump, Suze Orman, and Ron LeGrand, among others. Anthony has frequently been invited to speak at numerous REIC (real estate investing clubs) events throughout Southern California, Chicago, Florida, and New York.

In addition to his real estate career, Anthony is a nationally accredited USA girls fast pitch umpire, and he has umpired men's double A and triple A games. When he has time Anthony also loves to drag race on a quarter-mile track with his 1969 Camaro, which he helped build.

Anthony Patrick believes that almost anyone can succeed in real estate with the proper mentor, education, motivation, and passion. Transforming the lives of others and improving their quality of life is what Anthony is all about. Contact Anthony to find out how you can sign up for one of his weekend seminars held in Rancho Cucamonga, California, and learn for yourself the art of successful real estate investing.

www.NewHarvestVenturesLLC.com

It's Never Too Late

Ken and Barbara Tomayko

What would you do at age sixty if the company you had worked at for over twenty-five years decided to sell to one of its competitors? When Ken was faced with this dilemma, he and his wife, Barbara, decided to start a real estate investing business using their retirement funds.

This all happened over the course of one year, during which time Ken and Barbara worked their full-time jobs and on nights and weekends—with the help of family and a carpenter—they renovated and sold three homes. Ken recalls the day he was called in to the company president's office and told his job as chief financial officer was being eliminated. Ken's response was, "What took you so long?" The funny thing was that he was the only employee of 150 that had made any plans for the axe falling.

Over the next year, Ken worked full time on his real estate business, but instead of swinging a hammer, he hired a contractor and devoted his time to finding deals and the money to fund them. Then Ken and Barbara met Paul Finck and his team who challenged them to think bigger, and the dream transitioned from replacing Ken's salary and funding their retirement to creating the lasting legacy of a family business.

The immediate goal, as strongly stated by Barbara, was to enable her to leave her position as director of finance at the local United Way. The big challenge was that Barbara's employer did not seek a replacement, and Barbara continued to extend her employment on numerous occasions over a four-month period, which created stress for Ken, who was working eighteen-hour days attempting to keep up with their growing business. By this time their house renovating business had grown to over twenty combined renovations and buy-and-hold properties.

Finally, on October 31, 2012, Barbara left her job to join Ken in running the business. She was quickly followed by their oldest son, Brian, and his partner, Sinead, who moved back to Virginia to work with them. After a year of training, they have become integral members of the team. Brian and Sinead have been followed by Ken and Barbara's daughter, Kerry, her husband, James, and most recently by the youngest of their three children, Kevin, to form a true family business.

During the period from December 2011 to June 2017, the Tomaykos have renovated over 150 homes, accumulated forty single family rentals, and one thousand doors of self-storage. In the process they have developed numerous relationships with banks, realtors, and contractors, as well as other sundry real estate businesspeople, including an ongoing business relationship with Paul Finck's organization. This was all accomplished during a time when most people would have decided to retire.

Over the next couple of years, Barbara does plan on retiring, while Ken—who has real estate in his blood—plans to step back a bit and allow his children and their significant others to assume more control over the day-to-day operations.

The entire family has stepped up willingly and dynamically into their roles as business leaders, and the company is headed for a bright future. They have recently expanded into building new residential construction, which they feel is a business which will grow substantially in the coming years, and they continue to look for new opportunities.

KEN AND BARBARA TOMAYKO are the owners of B&K Properties, which they started to flip houses in 2009. They started this business as their "Plan B" when the company Ken had worked at for twenty-four years was sold and they knew it was only a matter of time until he would be out of a job.

They both have a strong faith and believe that God has a purpose and a reason for everything they do. One example is the night they were watching TV and an infomercial came on selling an education program on flipping houses. They thought, We can do this, so they purchased the program and studied all the material. After that they went looking for a realtor who understood the business they wanted to start, which was no easy task. However, they eventually found the right person, and the rest is history.

Their goal was and still is to create attractive, high-quality products for the end user. They have renovated over 150 homes, purchased forty-five rental properties, purchased two self-storage facilities with approximately one thousand doors, and they recently finished their first residential new home construction. They have been successful in obtaining over $1 million in investment capital through private investors. They also have formed great working relations with several community banks in their area.

As the business grew, it became very important to Ken and Barbara to be able to provide something for their children and give back to the community. All of their chil-

dren, along with their spouses or partners, now work for them. They have all become an integral part of the business and its success.

Both Ken and Barbara are very active in their communities. Ken was a coach for youth soccer for eleven years, coached youth basketball for four years, and was a youth soccer referee for five years. He has served on the council of his church as treasurer and president. He has volunteered on three different Habitat for Humanity projects. Ken is a member of his local Rotary Club, serving on several committees and currently president-elect. Barbara has volunteered at many of her children's schools, helping with different activities. She ran fundraising activities for soccer tournament and has served on her church council as treasurer. She currently is a member of the Lions Lioness Club in her community and has served as treasurer for this club; she also serves on the finance committee for a local nonprofit.

Ken and Barbara were both accountants in their previous occupations. Ken received his bachelor's degree in business from George Mason University, while Barbara received hers from Strayer University. In their careers Ken worked in the private sector, and Barbara worked in public accounting and nonprofit organizations.

CHANGE THE GAME

Paul Brown

Yes, I'll do it! That's what I nervously thought to myself, sitting in the middle of a real estate investors conference in Orlando. Yet I wasn't saying yes to real estate, or even the mentorship the speaker was pitching that morning back in early 2016. Ironically, I was saying yes to the needy, to what formerly felt like an impossible challenge, and to the most powerful and clear voice I've ever experienced.

Seemingly out of nowhere, God spoke to me during that seminar: "Paul, you're going to take responsibility for and fix the worldwide water problem in this generation." It was put to me with so much certainty that I knew it was basically already done. I confess, I was floored. And I believed it. And I accepted it. Getting sustainable systems of reliable water to the one in seven people that might die today because they don't have it became my "why," my driving purpose in life. This "why" rocked me to the core and completely changed me. Getting clear on my purpose is ultimately both how and why I am a Maverick today. Let me explain.

At the time, I was a tolerator. I tolerated abuse, an unfulfilled life, low pay, having my time owned by others, and a politely vague, not-on-purpose, quite un-designed life. Shortly after receiving my "why," I met Paul Finck, who quickly became a friend and mentor. He challenged me to change my story, my words, my friends, and my goals. Walking with him, I made these changes, which ultimately changed my results to the degree that I went from being on unemployment to building an annual six-figure residual income within six months. Here's how I did it.

I Changed My Story

I started saying "yes" and figuring it out as I went. No more "maybe" or "I'll think about it." I began showing up boldly, with high energy and ready to serve. This included acting as if: as if I was already a successful real estate investor. As if I had everything I needed. As if I had already won. I went ahead and internally identified with being a high-income earner *before* the deals and the deposits were made. And—you guessed it—I realized all of this shortly after I changed my identity and redesigned how I showed up.

My life literally changed forever when I first heard this quote by George Bernard Shaw. "People are always blaming their circumstances for what they are. I don't believe in circumstances. The people who get on in this world are the people who get up and look for the circumstances they want, and if they can't find them, *make* them."

The first creative real estate deal I completed was a result of this shift. A friend who I had helped in the past referred me to a homeowner named Jerry. He owed more on his house that it was worth, yet he wanted to move out of state immediately. An advisor told me there was really no way for me to help, and I passed this on to him. Then it hit me: "Paul, say yes and then figure it out!" I did. A week later, he and the buyer were thanking me profusely, and I was depositing a $15,000 check. Fifteen grand for three hours of helping people . . . that was the best wage I had earned yet, and it etched on my cortex the awesomeness of divorcing my then-life-long practice of trading of hours for dollars. So will you change your story? Say yes!

I Changed My Words

In addition to saying yes and many other positive affirmations, I eliminated *can't, try, working on it*, and *should*. I replaced if with when, but with and, and problem with challenge. This process had its challenges, yet the mental tension of catching myself before I spoke a negative word or correcting myself when I let one fly resulted in a change of mind, attitude, and action, not merely words. As the Book of Proverbs says, "Death and life are in the power of the tongue, and those who love it will eat its fruit." So what words will you choose?

I Changed My Friends

"You are the average of the five people you spend the most time with." When I first heard this saying from Jim Rohn, I was both saddened by my lack of successful friends and excited that now I had a specific way to design a better life. Yet one does not just snap one's fingers and make riffraff disappear and friends who are making quality choices appear. Ultimately I changed the composition of my associates via designed planning, being bold, and showing up to serve.

A year and a half ago, I had no friends who were millionaires. Now I have eight. How do you think that has affected my income? A month ago, I set some health goals. Since then, I've met five fit bodybuilders and added them to my life as friends. And like clockwork, I broke personal records on every exercise I do, blew through three-year plateaus in the gym, gave up junk food, and lost three inches off my waistline. Think that had anything to do with my new friends? Who will your friends be?

I Changed the Stakes

Getting reliable water to the poorest billion people is at least a 12 billion-dollar challenge. More immediately, I also realized that my three lovely children's futures were dependent on me achieving more. So I raised the stakes, dramatically increased my goals, and quickly made myself take bigger perceived risks. I decided to do whatever it takes. I stopped worrying about what could happen if I *do* and made myself aware of what will happen if I *don't*.

I've come to a place where I will not regret setbacks and snafus and will absolutely regret the "what ifs" bred by inaction. As Richard Branson says, "Sometimes the riskiest decision you can make is to do nothing." Playing it safe never is!

I stopped *playing not to lose* and started *playing to win*. This showed up most profoundly in three areas: 1) goal-setting; 2) investing large amounts of time and money on my training; and 3) becoming more comfortable with taking larger risks in real estate deals. Ironically, if I would have continued playing small, I would have lost big. So where will you raise the stakes?

Finding my "why" and getting clear on it has led me to make changes that have profoundly improved my life and the lives of my children, partners, clients, and friends. What's your "why"? Getting extremely clear about your driving life purpose, what grips you, is the first step in designing the life of your dreams. Yet, beyond merely challenging you to find your "why," I want to help you with it. The thing about "whys" is that they tend to be accomplished more effectively when we work together. Let's put our "whys" together and truly make it happen!

Connect with me on PaulBrownROI.com and share your "why" with me. Let's do this together. So are you ready? Now go change the game!

PAUL BROWN is a happy father of three beautiful, brilliant children. He founded Servant Leadership Charities in order to provide sustainable systems of reliable water for all people by 2034 in Jesus' name. Paul also runs Servant Leadership Properties in order to fund the expenses of the nonprofit by providing quality housing and creative real estate solutions for people in transition. In one short year, he has quickly become the local expert on quality

rooming houses and maximizing real estate profits. He lives in the Memphis, Tennessee, area, which he often refers to as Gotham City.

He enjoys making unexpected comments during meetings, as well as dancing, traveling, insinuating that he's Batman, speaking, working out, reading, writing, and spending time with and helping people. When Paul isn't engaged in the above, he is coaching his students in real estate investing and mind-set success, making funny remarks to strangers, or contemplating new strategies for friendly, gentle, and loving world domination. His favorite questions to ask others are: "What's your Why?" and "How may I help you?"

How can he help you?

PaulBrownROI.com

IMPROV AS A SPIRITUAL PRACTICE

Julie Cotton

Will you journey with me through a metaphor of choice? Choice, for me, is the doorway to freedom. And I associate freedom with success. The work (or rather play) that my life has been guiding me toward is that of an actor. My favorite technology for acting is improvisation. The following words are merely symbols exploring a perspective on the human condition. It is simply one of many methods I have discovered to open up joy, a willingness to connect, risk, fail, and succeed in every domain of life, such that I may lay my head to rest at the end of a fully expressed day and wake up ready to go at it all again upon the morn. Shakespeare said it best when he penned the immortal words, "All the world's a stage, and all the men and women merely players." May these next few pages invite you into your childlike wonder and sense of play—no matter what game(s) you may choose for your unique, vibrant, and successful life!

The Metaphor/Paradox: As the actor is not the character, so the Being is not the self. However, in both cases, the prior must come before that which follows. The one who notices is not the one who experiences. Many times, though, we confuse the two, even identifying as the experiences themselves. We are such good actors that we believe it to be true. The goal of any quality actor is to create truthful behavior in imaginary circumstances. So much so that the audience forgets that the world they are seeing—the story that is being presented—is not actually transpiring. We (as audience) become captured, captivated, and transfixed by what we witness when the skill of the actor transports us out of the here and now and submerges us into the world of their tale.

If we can teach novices to act with such truthfulness that they believe that their characters' created lives are their own, then can we not reversely teach the undoing of their very experience of existence?

Can we free the actor to create reality not solely on the stage, but in each one's own experience of life itself?

What then?

Observation becomes key. We learn the affliction of conditioning by observing others who have been afflicted. We see how it affects their bodies, behavior, beliefs,

51

interactions with their surroundings, etc. Then we look to mimic through the filter of our own instrument—body, voice, imagination.

We play and experiment. We alter our physical form, how and where we produce the sound of our voice, the filter through which we perceive information—and thus we can take on the likeness of another being—their history, belief system, thoughts, attitudes, mannerisms, the way they perceive the world—with a mere thought that causes a shift in energy within our own instrument. Amazing!

I can give myself a suggestion—character type, trait, personality, emotion, and so on—and transform . . . poof! Magic!

So why not do the same in our "real" lives? Why would it be any different ON stage versus OFF?

We created the worlds that we inhabit; why not change them? If we are in an experience of suffering, why not let that go? Call Black out. Curtain. End of Scene. Let the next scene come up to find an advance in time or consciousness where that suffering no longer exists for our characters.

Oh, but I have bills, a wife, kids, a job, responsibilities, obligations, people relying on me, duty, blah, blah, blah . . .

It is as you say it is. What we speak about we bring about, which merely compounds the issue.

A beautiful friend of mine, Carole Lynn Grant, said to me once, "We are what we say, so why not say something else?" She reminded me that, in the Bible, Jesus never spoke the problem.

Spiritual principles, such as the law of attraction, confirm that what we focus on grows and expands. Why not focus on beauty, peace, love, grace, simplicity, health, fun, laughter, or truly anything we love?

Human beings too often are drawn to thoughts of pain and suffering like a moth to a flame. The challenge of the human condition is that we are so identified with our suffering that without it, our story would_____ (fill in the blank).

Many of us can't imagine a life without suffering. Suffering is synonymous with separation. Ego has the role and obligation of reminding us of our separateness—from each other, from the Divine/Source, from our circumstances, you name it. It's part of the game of being humans. We agree: OK, I accept this role; I will wear this costume; I will assume these characteristics and personality traits until the end of the play. Ego's role is essential in the play. Without it, the human story itself would come to a screeching halt. Ego in and of itself is not bad. It is a function of the form. No ego, no body, no human experience.

It is when we let ego direct the play that the individual characters experience more suffering than necessary.

I am not saying, "Let's not be human." There is so much beauty in humanity. But why not experience the beauty as the actor, not the character? There are times when I have gotten so caught up in playing a role that I've lost myself in the character. Caught up in the moment, I've actually experienced the emotions the character is feeling; the lines of the script no longer seeming to have been prewritten. In and of itself, this is not a bad thing—it's often what makes the audience leap to its feet at the end of the performance. But at the end of the day, we must always remember that we are the actor; we are creating the action on the set. In real life too, we are the chooser choosing; circumstances are not just happening randomly to us without our control.

In this metaphor, the play does not end. It's not eight shows a week. Our scenes keep arising. Our roles evolve and change as different characters, locations, relationships present themselves, streaming together to form the story of our lives. Our individual character may alter, evolve, or change as we are met with new circumstances, epiphanies, catharses. But the play continues until we lay aside our human meat suit of a costume and are reunited with the Divine.

If this conversation resonates with you and you are interested in playing with the freedom improv can guide you toward, please connect with me at nextlevelimprov. com or reach out to your local improv companies. Begin the exploration of play, laughter, and choice as a gateway to your next level of freedom and success!

JULIE COTTON, a native of Phoenix, Arizona, has been an actor for over thirty years and a healer/ bodyworker since 2007. She has performed in more than seventy-five improv comedy, stage productions, corporate shows, touring shows, voiceovers, industrials, educational videos, and independent films. She earned her MFA in Acting from Rutgers MGSA and holds a BA in Theater-Emphasis in Education and Vocal Performance from Grand Canyon University. You can see Julie on Nickelodeon's 2016 show Talia in the Kitchen as Aunt Tilly. She co-facilitated at the ADEC 2016 Conference on How to Use Improv in Grief and Loss Therapy. She is a graduate of Trainer Designs Global Trainer Forum and a trainer for Improv for Beginners, Acting and Authenticity, and TransActing with Gratitude Training LLC. She founded Next Level Improv, LLC, where she leads Transformational Improv Therapy at recovery facilities, Acting Techniques for Graduate Professors in Mathematics at Princeton, Improv Levels 1–5, How to Teach Improv, and Corporate

Team Building Trainings. Julie is a licensed massage therapist, CranioSacral therapist, VortexHealing practitioner, certified Pilates instructor, and second-degree black belt in American Kickboxing. She enjoys applying healing and theater arts in transformational ways and stands for a world that is loving, joyful, and free!

Probate 101 for Real Estate Investors

Paul Wilkins

"In this world nothing can be said to be certain except death and taxes." This is one of many words of wisdom spoken by Benjamin Franklin. While there are many resources to assist you with the latter, this chapter will assist real estate investors with the former. Despite the forethought of many individuals who prepare wills, any real property held outside of trust will be subject to probate—the legal process by which assets are transferred from the deceased owner to his or her heirs. Many people assume that the existence of a will precludes the need for probate. Unfortunately, that assumption is incorrect.

Now, some good news for real estate investors! Thanks to the probate process, there is a constant, steady stream of millions of investment properties going through probate each year throughout the US. Wherever people live and die, there will be probates, period. Since people die in all fifty states and in every nation on earth, there will be countless millions of properties always available for resale.

Good estate planners can often assist their clients to avoid probate through a trust. However, a trust is not necessarily a perfect defense. If the trust document is lost, or if there are disputes concerning the trust after the death or incapacity of the trust settlor (the person who establishes the trust), these matters will end up in probate court—the very venue the trust settlors hoped to avoid in the first place!

One benefit of investing in probate properties is that this niche is never out of vogue. For example, after the financial crisis of 2007–2008, there were millions of REO homes on the market. However, there were many fewer real estate investors back then, because most people were scared and could not see the bottom of the market. Those of us who are seasoned real estate professionals saw how low the market had dropped and began buying at a frenzied pace. By 2010–2011, the supply of REOs had dwindled rapidly and dropped even further as big Wall Street investors dove into the market and purchased tens of thousands of homes.

Another investment niche that was in favor shortly after the financial crisis of 2008 was short sales. Short sales occurred when property values fell below previous appraised levels and could not be sold for a sufficiently high price to pay the existing loan in full. In most cases the homeowners lacked the liquidity to cover this negative spread between the deflated value and loan balance, and so requested their lenders to approve the sale for less than the outstanding loan balance—hence the nickname "short" sale. Real estate agents, whose livelihoods were negatively impacted by the stifled real estate market, now received some relief.

This investment sector faded into the sunset once the US Justice Department and other federal and state agencies extracted billions of dollars in concessions from the major money center banks for their alleged abuses and mismanagement of real estate borrowers during the financial crisis. Instead of paying the federal and state governments these multibillion-dollar settlements in cash, the majority of payments were made via credits given to homeowners who were delinquent or in foreclosure. These credits allowed the banks to either reduce interest rates and/ or loan balances, or defer loan payments to the end of the loan. The combination of these remedies provided qualified homeowners with some form of loan relief. This action immediately eliminated the need for the banks to approve short sales, as now the banks were required to "spend" these concessions on their existing customers needing assistance. Rather than approve short sales and see those loans disappear forever, the new incentives for loan modifications provided the banks with the opportunity to recapture lost income via these recast loans. The modified loans would be less profitable than those they replaced, but these loans were still profitable—and still on the books. Whereas REOs and short sales have come and gone, probate opportunities remain.

I have earned my livelihood over the past twenty-plus years as a result of probate transactions. When I first started, I literally knew nothing about probate. Now, after nearly twenty-one years of experience, you can gain much of this knowledge through the lessons in my forthcoming book, *Probate For Real Estate Investors*. I interact daily with numerous probate attorneys and paralegals in California and many other states. Their information and assistance has added value to my knowledge, which now can become your knowledge. I learn something new every single day— not because I don't know much, but because there is so much information in each state's Probate Code, local court rules, and so forth.

My purpose is to provide you with all requisite information to succeed in probate investing without having to spending the next twenty-plus years that I have already invested in the field. I sincerely want you to achieve financial success, as many of my previous students have. My hope is that I can assist you to achieve monetary success in the near future, and possibly work together with you in future financially rewarding transactions too!

Since people are always dying, there will always be an endless source of probate leads. For example, let's say that you wanted to concentrate only on Los Angeles County for prospects. If, for some inexplicable reason, probate leads or investment opportunities were to dry up in Los Angeles County, you could switch your efforts to an adjacent county, be it Orange, San Bernardino, or Riverside Counties. Again, even if one county were to become temporarily unproductive, there would be no reason that other adjacent or nearby counties would be so afflicted. And should an entire state become less productive or totally unproductive (due to significant changes to the probate laws), you could move your efforts to another nearby state.

Personally, Arizona has provided me with several probate investment opportunities over the past few years. The point remains that you will never get tired nor bored while pursuing probate leads, as these "wells" will never completely run dry.

I've used the probate laws and procedures in California as the basis of the information provided in this chapter. Since forty-nine of the fifty states base their laws on English Common Law (Louisiana, based on French Law, being the only exception), the probate codes and practices in most states are parallel to each other. Over the years in my probate business, that has certainly been true; there are many more similarities than differences between the English Common Law states.

Once you understand the process, you should be able to review and extract the requisite information for each case in five minutes or less. At this rate, you can easily gather ten to twelve probate cases—your new leads—per hour. This is true whether the research is done at the court or online. As part of your initial probate education, you may want to do the research yourself. Once you master this skill, you can hire an assistant to gather this data. If you pay this assistant ten to twelve dollars per hour, your cost per lead is roughly a dollar. This is very affordable, especially since this is proprietary information that you are not sharing with anyone else.

Other real estate investing niches, such as foreclosure and bankruptcy, may provide database subscriptions at a lower price per lead, but that information is sold to fifty to one hundred investors each time. The value of your probate data, at a dollar per lead, can and will prove valuable over time. Since your probate competition is minimal, your results should be very cost-effective when compared to other investors who rely on the aforementioned shared information.

Successful probate investing has a low cost of entry, and then, once you have the necessary information information, the only additional cost is the amount of a postage stamp. No costly software or monthly subscriptions are necessary for probate investing, unlike other investing niches. And sometimes the cost can even be less than a postage stamp. A few courts list phone numbers on the basic probate forms. Some of my students found the administrator's phone number during the course of their research, took the initiative, and picked up the phone. In less than ten days, they had the estate property under contract, and within thirty days they received a wholesale fee of $18,000! For the cost of a phone call, these students did quite well—especially since they put up zero dollars to secure the deal!

Probate is a profitable investment niche that can be pursued everywhere. By following the principles I clearly outline for you, you'll be able to get started without any previous experience. With an endless stream of leads, minimal research costs, and nominal costs to start your career as a probate investor, you'll soon be on your own path to success. For additional information, feel free to contact me at paul@probateinvestingbook.com.

 *PAUL WILKINS' initial career objective was to be an educator. He earned both a BA (magna cum laude) and a MA in History from the University of California, Los Angeles (UCLA). After spending two summers as an intern for a local commercial bank, his new interest in banking spurred him to earn a MBA from the Anderson School at UCLA. After graduation he entered the credit training program at Bank of America. Subsequent jobs provided additional experiences as an REO manager for a multibillion dollar mortgage lender, regional portfolio manager for a major private mortgage insurer, and a stint as a Liquidation Specialist for the Federal Deposit Insurance Corporation (FDIC). He concluded his financial services tour of duty with two regional commercial banks, handling both commercial real estate workouts and REOs.*

Paul's professional fun really began in 1996, when he joined National Consumers Finance Company, which later changed its name to Heir Buyout Company. Working on an average of over fifty probate cases per month, Paul has gained substantial knowledge of the probate process over the past twenty-one years. In 2010 he and his business partners founded what is now Approved Inheritance Cash, a national provider of credit during the probate process.

GET UP, DRESS UP, SHOW UP, AND NEVER GIVE UP

Sinéad Sanderson

I have always chosen my own path, taken risks, and done things outside of the norm. I didn't go to university, I knew from a young age that I was never going to have children, I moved continents at the age of twenty-four, and got married in Las Vegas. I have always done whatever it takes, worked long hours, and kept moving, despite many setbacks—including suffering from several autoimmune and mental illnesses. I am still not where I want to be, yet, but I have gone from bartending to being the acquisitions manager in a multimillion-dollar company in less than five years. I have never given up, and I never will give up on my dreams.

I put in, on average, seventy hours a week at work. In my spare time, I pursue my personal goal of being an artist. I have found that I feel unfulfilled and more stressed when I don't focus any time on my art, so in early 2017 I set up an Etsy site to sell my jewelry, greeting cards, and collages, which I make using upcycled materials where possible. The site has been encouragingly successful so far, and in June 2017 I was also invited to be a showcase artist at a local art gallery. It is my goal to open my own art gallery in the next ten years. As far as I am concerned, the real estate business is a means to an end to achieve my goals.

I suffer from a connective tissue disease, lymphocytic colitis, fibromyalgia, bi-polar disorder, anxiety, and OCD. I am always in pain, always fatigued, and always dealing with brain fog. Some days it is extremely difficult just to get out of bed, let alone work seventy-plus hours a week in a very stressful job, especially when I live so far away from my support network of friends and family back home. But I do it. Don't get me wrong, I have bad days, but I refuse to let these issues define me or keep me from my dreams. Some days I have to take a breath, step back, and look at how far I've come. My motto is: "Get Up, Dress Up, Show Up, and NEVER GIVE UP."

I did not have the easiest adolescence; I was bullied for many years and suffered from severe depression from a young age. I was a good student, but I knew I did not want to go to university, and I knew I didn't want four-plus years of extra education in art, which was my desired vocation. I knew how expensive that would work out to be and what little chance I actually had of getting an art-related job at the end of it. I started working in retail at age sixteen, not really knowing what else to do with my life at the time. I saved enough money to go backpacking around Egypt when I was nineteen, because I had always been fascinated by Egyptian history and mythology, and I had always wanted to travel. After that I went back to retail, and became the manager of the local branch of a high-profile national card shop at the age of twenty-two.

Around that same time, I had started dating an older American man. After three years together, his job wanted him back in the States, so I followed him to Virginia, where I began bartending. We got married in Las Vegas, with no friends or family to witness it. I left behind all my friends, family, and everything I had ever known to be with him. Unfortunately, our marriage ended up being very abusive. I had a complete breakdown and attempted suicide. Against the odds, I survived, but while I was in the hospital, my husband filed for divorce. I had another mental relapse, but eventually I came to realize how unhealthy our relationship had been, and how much better off I would be without him.

Soon after getting out of the hospital, I had a rebound fling that turned into the love of my life. My partner, Brian, is a fellow artist, and I moved from Virginia to Washington, D. C., to be with him. After two years together, we made the decision to relocate to Albuquerque, New Mexico in 2010, spending all our savings to move out there. The plan was to open an art gallery together, but once there, we found out what a recession actually looked like. The last thing people were willing to spend money on was art. However, people always eat and drink, no matter the current financial market, so, I ended up bartending again. In 2012 Brian's parents invited us to join their real estate investment business. They had just started working with Paul Finck and had plans to expand their modest business model to something much grander. Not having found what we were looking for in New Mexico, Brian and I packed everything up once again, and once again spent all our savings to move across the county to try something new.

After a couple of months of training with the Tomaykos, they bought a program that focused on HUD houses, and I was given the task of putting bids on HUD houses in Virginia. Within two weeks it became abundantly clear to me that the model they bought wouldn't work in our market. So I adapted it for Virginia, and it became my more-than-full-time job to research and bid on HUD houses in the area. Within four weeks I had created a system that worked in our market, and it is now our most successful model for finding properties to rehab or rent. Over 70 percent of the houses we have worked on in the last five years have been the result of my work. Not bad for someone who was completely unfamiliar with computers before this! I went from being barely able to check my email to designing spreadsheets and innovating property research systems in the space of one month. For the last four and a half years, I have spent seventy-plus hours, seven days a week, working on property research, HUD, and marketing our houses through social media. It has not been easy, but it has paid off! Recently I also studied for and got my own real estate license. B&K Properties now has a net worth of over $10 million, having expanded from residential to commercial ventures, and just this year we've added new construction to our rehab and rental businesses.

Thank you for reading my story. I hope it may inspire you to get out there and pursue your dreams, no matter your fears and setbacks. We all deserve to live the life we've always imagined, and I am so grateful to those who have helped me on my journey so far.

SINÉAD SANDERSON is an artist, jewelry maker, and real estate entrepreneur. Born and raised in England, Sinéad moved to the United States at twenty-four and currently lives in Virginia. After working in multiple retail and service industry jobs on two continents, in 2012 Sinéad was given the opportunity to join B&K Properties (see separate chapter on the Tomaykos). She is now the acquisitions manager for this highly successful family real estate team, and the systems and procedures she designed have counted for 70 percent of the residential growth of the business. In 2017 Sinéad also got her own real estate license.

Sinéad has never given up on her goals of becoming a successful artist, and over the years she has had personal and commercial commissions from people, pubs, and even rock bands. In early 2017 Sinéad started her own online Etsy shop to sell jewelry, and she has been working on expanding her social media reach, which grew over 1,200 percent in the first six months. In June 2017 Sinéad was also invited to be a showcase artist at an art gallery in Hampton, Virginia. It is her goal to open her own gallery in the next ten years.

https://www.etsy.com/shop/OriginalSinArt
https://www.facebook.com/OriginalSinArt/
https://www.instagram.com/originalsinart/
https://www.pinterest.com/OriginalSinArt/

Rocketman—Pedaling to Paradise

Kevin Vibert

Two years into the real estate wholesaling business, and I was going nowhere. Sure, I had made some money (averaging $30K a year is not bad for part time); I had made a couple of big scores and a couple of small ones, but it wasn't going to get me where I was looking to go—i.e., paradise. It wasn't that I didn't have a goal or even that I didn't have a plan; I had the resemblance of both. But something was missing. There was something I just wasn't grasping. I was doing the business in fits and flats, there was no continuum, and I could not see any progress toward my goals.

Then it came to me in a vision. I'm not talking about a religious vision—I didn't see God pointing the way or anything like that. What I'm talking about is the way I "get" stuff in mental pictures and videos. On the screen in my head, I saw "Rocketman" trying to glide out of orbit only to be pulled back into his CZ (Comfort Zone) by its enormous CZP (Comfort Zone Pull), a gravitational-like force. There are few forces in life greater than the Comfort Zone; we all have one. It's that point in your personal reality where you have accepted the conditions and limitations of your personal daily life as comfortable. Even though you may have the desire to move beyond it to bigger and better things, you find it very hard to justify the effort and discomfort it would take to get there.

So back to Rocketman—he's got the rocket of desire strapped to his back and is committed to head for a new CZ somewhere out there in space. He knows it's real because he's seen it from afar, way out there in the sky. Don't think for a minute it's been easy for him to get this far, though! All the equipment and training necessary just to launch has brought forth every naysayer in his CZ. "Are you cray cray?" "What about us!" He's already fighting the CZP, but he's committed; he's ready to blast off.

10 . . . 1—BLASTOFF!

It's a spectacular launch—the initial acceleration is phenomenal! The rockets stop as the fuel of desire only goes so far, and Rocketman is now in orbit, closer than ever before to his new and vastly improved CZ but unable to get there. He begins to measure his results. He did have some success, but all the cost and effort to launch only got him this far and no further. In fact, without any sustained action capabilities, he begins to descend back to his original CZ.

Rocketman's not giving up, though. With time to think about his next attempt, he analyzes his trip and comes to this conclusion: "While the rocket of desire was enough to get me into orbit around my CZ, it will not be enough to break free of CZP. The real work doesn't start until you hit orbit, and then you must put in enough extra effort to break out of orbit and move toward your new desired CZ." While no one's analysis can tell him exactly how much effort will be necessary to break out of CZP, he knows that once he does, his new desired CZ will begin to pull him along.

Back in his comfort zone now, there are many well-meaning and not so well-meaning friends and family that will find a need to express their "told you so" opinion one way or another. Rocketman has no time for that! He is back in his workshop designing his rocket ship for his next attempt at breaking out of his CZ. Realizing that while the rocket of desire will get him into orbit, it will be up to him to put in the continuous extra effort to break free from CZP. How much extra effort? *WHATEVER IT TAKES! IT WILL BE A LOT, IT WILL BE UNCOMFORTABLE, AND IT WILL BE CONTINUOUS!* Rocketman adds a pedal-driven propeller to his rocket of desire, and to his Ops Manual he adds the following new words of instruction:

1. ACTION def: A combination of new "whatever it takes" effort and discomfort sufficient enough to break free of your previous CZ and propel you to your desired CZ. Note: Not to be confused with working hard at what you are already comfortable with.
2. Once launched:
   a. Apply continuous and unrelenting ACTION to the pedals. Do not stop until you are in orbit around the CZ of your DESIRE.
   b. Do not stop to measure the distance you need to go to get to the CZ of your desire; it doesn't matter! Keep pedaling! It is sufficient to know you are staying securely in the UCZ (Un-Comfort Zone), getting farther away from the CZ you are leaving.
   c. If you are not feeling uncomfortable, pedal harder— adjust something and pedal even harder!
   d. Measure your ACTION! Ask yourself: Am I really pedaling harder? Am I in the new and uncomfortable? Is it time to switch to the next gear?

Ships Log (a time in the future): As I have progressed out into the uncomfortable unknown, it is becoming apparent that the Comfort Zone I was running from has grown and now contains many things for me that were once uncomfortable and seemed unattainable. This was not what I expected. I thought I was moving to a new CZ, but now I realize that the continuous action that keeps me in the UCZ has expanded my universe and creates—without any additional effort—a larger, richer, and more social CZ than I ever could have imagined. A paradise perfect for landing and refueling and getting ready for the next level of expansion!

Signing off for now,

Rocketman!

KEVIN VIBERT was born to Eileen Mary (Hawkes) and John Witherspoon Vibert on May 31st, 1955, in Hartford, Connecticut. The sixth of eleven Vibert children, Kevin would come to be considered the quintessential middle child. Growing up in Unionville, Connecticut, a small, middle-class industrial/farming community along the great Farmington River, in the house his father had also grown up in, Kevin understood the importance of hard work and financial income when he was quite young. By age eight he oversaw the delivery and collections of one of the five Vibert/Hartford Courant paper routes. Over the next ten years, Kevin learned many lessons in teamwork and leadership from his parents and siblings as he worked toward his own entrepreneurial dreams of success. At eighteen Kevin graduated from high school and joined the United States Air Force, beginning a four-year tour of duty as a C130 Aircraft Crew Chief. Having earned an honorable discharge in 1977 in Honolulu, Hawaii, Kevin contemplated island life for several months, but ultimately big-family ties would bring him back to Connecticut and a new career as a computer systems consultant. For the next thirty years Kevin lived and worked in many cities in the US, returning once again to Connecticut to raise his late-in-life daughters, India and Asia, five miles from where he grew up. He is now working on his next life project: Unchained Financial Success, designed to cut the ties between time and money.

Rad Ways

Patrick Kluge

My career started as a child who had a fascination with what makes things work. Experimenting and taking anything and everything apart and repairing broken radios and televisions in the basement of our house was the start of my electronics career.

My first job was in TV repair at the age of fourteen in 1974, prior to any formal training. My job was actual repair work. I will always be grateful to Jack Luskin ("The Cheapest Guy in Town") for my start.

Mentors appeared—these were the technicians in the shop that did not want to fix the black-and-white TVs. Color TVs were "the thing," and the other technicians must have felt it was better to teach the "Kid" rather than do it themselves. A vocational technical high school was my choice for electronics training, followed by some college. Component level repairs were necessary for the technology at that time and established my deep troubleshooting roots.

I got bored with TV repair after a few years and needed a new challenge. I transitioned into hospital equipment repair for a medical supply company. I was a learning sponge. Six months into my new job, my boss, Bob, traumatized me: He opened the shop door and rolled a piece of equipment in with a Red Service Manual on top of it. All he said was, "Pat, you need to do a 10,000-hour overhaul on this system by the end of the week," and walked away. The panic started instantly!

To make a long story short, I wrote the book on how to perform a 10,000-hour overhaul on this particular life-support system. This type of training is not the norm today, yet it is still the best training bar none. After realizing that I was grossly underpaid, I moved on to a two-hundred-bed hospital. I was their only biomedical technician. This is a seemingly undervalued but important role in a hospital, similar to the Maytag repairman. This hospital was so huge to me that it seemed like a small city. I realized my boundaries quickly and felt like a trapped animal that needed space. I made the transition from working in the hospital to my first of three manufacturer field positions.

I worked for two ultrasound imaging manufacturers and a leading surgical X-ray imaging manufacturer as a senior field service engineer. Each manufacturer having their own product-specific service training programs became the next level of my education. I have been to Australia, Brazil, Japan, and Europe, performing service and training in a specialist's role. This journey and technical growth started from the TV repair shop in 1974 and continued through 2008 when I left the corporate world and started Rad Rays LLC.

Toward the end of my corporate career, I decided to learn real estate investing, which is continually ongoing for me. I rehabbed a property and sold it for a substantial gain while working at my corporate job. I could never have made as much in overtime pay as I did completing this real estate transaction from start to finish. Fortunately, I sold the property just before the 2007 real estate crash. The proceeds continued to fund my real estate training, which gave me the much-needed business knowledge to continue on two paths: real estate investing and Rad Rays.

During the last year of my corporate existence, I had five weeks of vacation that I used for real estate training seminars, which typically were held two, three, or four days at a time. The passion to better myself and reposition myself was huge. The entrepreneurial spirit as well as the need to leave the nine-to-five job world created an immense internal struggle.

Due to increased pressures of my day job, I felt stress that was excessive, demotivating, and unnecessary. I felt like I was "going postal"—i.e going nuts on the job. This stress was the final straw as well as the needed push to break the barrier and get out of my job. It was a quantum leap for me to break through the "employee to business owner" barrier.

My tenure with the X-ray manufacturer was from 1993 to 2008, and since then Rad Rays has given me many learning opportunities. I continue to learn more about the equipment that I know so well, and I've experienced tremendous business and personal growth. In my company, we share knowledge amongst ourselves to keep our combined skills honed. We have an excellent team, full of people with integrity who enjoy the challenging environment. There is never a dull day.

Real estate training has enabled me to further my future plans by growing both paths, X-ray imaging and real estate investing. It is interesting to note the number of similarities in the business models between real estate investing and an X-ray service company. For example, wholesale and retail are components of both industries. The terminology may be different but is still very similar—such as "rehabbed" versus "refurbished."

Rad Rays is in constant growth mode. We specialize in one brand of surgical C-arms spanning several models, and we train our technicians in house.

We are a company that operates in a niche market, providing service, specialist-level service, technical support, parts sales, rental equipment, and used and refurbished system sales. We are small and mighty. Our goal is to provide the highest quality parts, service, support services, and equipment.

We have a very loyal customer base. While we may not be the least expensive, we provide value that you won't get anywhere else. The same-day fix is one of our specialties. By having local parts support along with well-trained, skilled technicians, we can lower equipment downtime and repair costs and thus avoid the rescheduling of patient procedures. I believe and instill the values of old-fashioned customer service that is fast becoming a lost art due to the internet and handheld electronics.

In closing, I asked my team members to comment about what they thought about me and why they like working at Rad Rays. There was an immense amount of positive feedback about my traits as well as why they are engaged. This exercise taught me how much they appreciate me because I appreciate them, care for them, train them professionally, and help them personally. The family feel, the joking, friendly environment, and the camaraderie with mutual respect overall is key. I am proud of my guys stepping up to the plate and answering me truthfully. No suggestion box can do this. Rad Rays uses this video as part of our internal training: https://www.youtube.com/watch?v=bPHAPFYhKwQ.

There are so many parallels between Maytag and Rad Rays. That's why I'm giving my team a history lesson to reinforce our values. By now you should know why "Rad Ways" is what drives Rad Rays.

 *Patrick (Pat) Kluge is a businessman in the medical equipment sector. He started as a child with a fascination of what made things work. His father gave him a book that was treasured, simply titled* How Things Work *(1960's version). Pat would like to dedicate this chapter of the book to his father, Ino Karl Kluge, who encouraged him to learn the skills that interested him—specifically electronics—at a young age. His father knew that it was best to assist Pat to get to the environment that was needed to thrive in rather than impeding his growth. Ino was an artist as well as a professional in the field of international sales and marketing. His mother, Jana, on the other hand, wanted a son who would be a doctor or a lawyer. (She's gotten over that by now.) Pat has always been passionate about electronics and is happy that his parents' support allowed him to follow the electronics path early on. He has trained several high-caliber technicians and will continue to do so.*

www.RadRays.com

"We Are the OEC Specialists"

God Is My Real Estate Agent

Brenda Hayward

Have you ever looked back to a traumatic period in your life and noticed the way God was setting things up so the terrible things that would happen will be of value—so you will be lifted and supported in ways you cannot see until later?

It started with Mom. She felt she couldn't breathe because of the pollution in the air. When she finally agreed to go to the doctor, she found that she had cancer for the *third* time. This time it was lymphoma, a fast-growing cancer that, in her case, was centered on her esophagus and lungs and strangling her to death. It was inoperable. Her chemo treatments started immediately, and her breathing started to improve. But when the treatment caused a stroke, I left my children and my husband, Don, and headed to Canada to be with her for a while.

When I got back home, I discovered that I was pregnant with child number nine. I had forgotten to take my birth control pills with me and never even thought about it while I was with my mom. I wasn't thrilled, but I knew this baby would be loved just as we loved the others.

Then we got some great news. Mom recovered quickly from the stroke, and her cancer went into remission. She and my dad moved closer to family, and we could see her often. We loved it.

Now the Lord stepped in—because he had some plans.

My husband and I purchased a lot and eight acres of pasture land, and we were getting ready to build on the lot. Don mentioned our plans at work, and one Saturday some people showed up at our home and asked if they could see it. They walked through, asked how much, we picked a price, and they gave us some earnest money. We now had until July 1st to move.

We were stunned. We had just sold our house! We had to move *fast!* Building a house takes all the time you will give it.

The problem was that nothing was working with the building lot. The house I wanted to build was just outside our price range, and when the builder saw the lot, which was on a hill, it dramatically increased the price. I didn't want to pour my

71

heart and soul into building a house I didn't want, so we made an offer on a six-acre farm with an existing house. The Lord stepped in, and I sold the lot that weekend to someone who just "happened" to want that particular lot, and I sold the pasture land the next week. Everything dropped into place so fast it was dazzling. Selling our home, lot, and pasture and "buying" the farm took less than two weeks. All we had to do now was close on everything and pack.

I can't begin to tell you everything that miraculously happened—there isn't space in this chapter. But God had a specific place for us to be in order to be ready for what was coming.

You see, Mom's cancer came back hard and fast. They had said that it might, and they also told us there was no treatment left. And then on June 15, one week before my due date, my obstetrician couldn't find a heartbeat. I just stared at him. I was so calm I surprised myself. He took me into his office and handed me his phone so I could have some privacy as I called Don. I dialed his number, and when I heard Don's voice I calmly told him Kaitlyn was gone—and *then* I broke down. It wasn't real until that moment. We found out later that Kaitlyn must have died the night before.

My sister had buried an infant with birth defects two years before and graciously allowed us to place our little girl in the same plot. The mortuary gave us a free casket for the burial. My mom came to the funeral, but it was the last time she left her apartment. Her systems were shutting down. She held on until her oldest brother arrived, and then she was gone on July 1. We had just finished moving to the farm, two weeks to the day after Kaitlyn died. I kept busy unpacking and thought I was handling it really well.

But if I was handling it so well, why did I quit H&R Block after eight years just after I had been promoted to manage a satellite office for them? Why did I stop singing? I continued to function, but the joy was gone. It took time, but I discovered that the Lord had given me a healing place in this farm with amazing people to support me.

I will always be grateful because of the peace and freedom and the wonderful people we found there. Three of my children met their spouses there. Don was laid off, and we were able to provide most of what we needed until he was employed again. I was able to start several small businesses, and I reveled in the freedom of our six acres.

We lived there for five years until the Lord decided it was time for a new adventure in another state. He sold our house for us again. I knew it was coming and had sold off my small business ventures before it happened. Then a job offer for Don came out of the blue. He wasn't even looking. And before we got an agent, we had an offer on the farm. Has anyone else had the Lord as their real estate agent? I would love to know. I have sold several homes and have never had time to put a sign in the yard.

I have learned so much in the twenty-five years since that fateful month.

I have learned that service to others is one of the greatest healing balms known to mankind. It takes you out of yourself and your needs and allows you to focus on others and what they need. It is like a dot on a white sheet of paper. If you hold that dot in front of your eyes, it fills your vision and is huge. The more you focus on your own issues and challenges, the less you can see around you until they become consuming and overwhelming. The only solution is to back up, look around, and find something positive to focus on outside of yourself. Serving others does all this.

I have learned that I cannot do it alone. I need the help of others, and I have learned to ask for it.

I have learned persistence and determination, forgiveness and generosity. I have learned that I am stronger than I give myself credit for.

I have studied the Scriptures and learned once again that there is a time for everything. A time to be born, a time to die; a time to weep, a time to laugh; a time to mourn, and a time to dance; a time to break down, and a time to build up.

Most importantly, I have learned to give back because I have been given so very, very much.

Oh, and I have learned that God is an amazing RE agent!

BRENDA HAYWARD is a real estate investor, certified Bankcode trainer, entrepreneur, and coach. She has been happily married to the same man for forty-three years. She loves traveling and visiting her ninety-three-year-old father and eighty-eight-year-old mother-in-law as well as her eight surviving children and their spouses, twenty-four grandchildren, and one great-grandchild. Over the years she has served her church in the women's organization, led the choir, taught religious education, led the Activities Committee, worked with the Boy Scouts, and more. She loves to paint, create Christmas ornaments, start small businesses, and help women see their own greatness and achieve their dreams.

Universal Sales Hacks

Benjamin Chatson

When it comes to sales, I have been at opposite ends of the spectrum, and both sides of the table. For years now, I have been a consistently high- performing salesperson. Prior to that, I worked as an outside technician for Bellsouth now AT&T. I can easily say that I understand and can completely relate to the dislike for pushy, manipulative salespeople, and I totally get the fear or aversion to selling for a living.

I wandered into the sales seminars/personal development arena around 2009, while I was still at AT&T. I bought in all the way. I spent many thousands of dollars on trainings and additional seminars, and eventually I felt like I got duped by salespeople who were only interested in getting money out of me. I blamed them when I did not succeed right away. However my path was exactly what I needed to find myself here, writing this for you.

I spent the next few years doing additional types of mind-set trainings, and approximately a year and a half ago, I completed my transformational trainer certification with Trainer Designs Global. Now, just attaining the certification doesn't really mean anything. Already having been in sales for a few years, the training opened me up to the larger possibility of designing and sharing learned concepts. I learned these from others, as well innovating new and fresh ideas based on my experiences and personal path through the sales and life arena. At this point, my goal is to support entrepreneurs and businesses that have a fear of selling, or an aversion to it. I assist them to understand that sales is part of what they need to engage in in order to successfully break away from working for someone else, go after what they want and elevate their business. When everyone has sales skills, we will never suffer from a bad economy and will always be able to provide for ourselves and loved ones. That's not a bad thing.

My first sales mentor a few years ago said to me, "Sales is the most spiritual practice you can engage in." While that sounded good, I didn't really understand what that meant at first. From where I stand now, I completely agree. Being in sales has taught me more about myself and others than almost any other experience in my life. I've learned what holds me back, what holds others back, and what stands in our way, especially where money is involved. Unfortunately, money tends to be what trips everyone up in the sales process. Highly effective salespeople that do a great job by their clients have the ability to caringly move the focus off the money. Instead of putting emphasis on and around money, they place the focus on everything else that is important to the client so the exchange of money becomes a natural and comfortable result.

Discovering the Universal Sales Hacks

Universals Sales Hacks are designed to bridge the gap of time and experience for someone who possibly feels stuck in a job not believing anything else is possible and not great at sales or doesn't even like it. They tremendously shorten the learning curve to my present day level of experience, so you can stand where I stand, and see what I see. Consistent success and improvement tend to follow.

Let's work backwards. What's a *hack*? In the movie *The Matrix* (1999), the main character, Neo, was a computer hacker. If you read between the lines, he was probably the best hacker ever. This is what allowed him to do the things he did inside the Matrix, such as bend the external environment to his will with his intention. Of course, this was only possible once he chose the red pill, and woke up from a lifelong sleep of being a slave to the system. Two of my favorite quotes from the movie are:

> "What you must learn is that these **rules** are no different than **rules** of a computer system. Some of them can be bent; others can be **broken**."

> "**I can only show you** the door. You're the one that has to walk through it. "

Traditionally, a "hack" breaks into a system or network that is seemingly otherwise impenetrable to change the results in someone's favor much like the security breaches when corporations lose our personal information.

In our context, sales is the system we are hacking. We are hacking into the system, looking around, and inserting new programming, code, or language. We are transforming the hard problems into fluid solutions. As we smooth out the process we become more effective, practical, and relatable all at the same time.

Universal? Well, that has more than one meaning. These hacks are meant to be universally applicable for all. My intention is for the hacks I am sharing with you to be practical and immediately usable. They have been developed and revolved around the most common sales topics, such as:

- Assuming the Sale
- Transitioning to Close
- Asking for the Sale
- Overcoming Objections and Rebuttals
- Controlling the Call

You can find much more on my website, www.UniversalSalesHacks.com.

I upgrade these traditional concepts for our current level of consciousness in a very practical and real way. We shift the language around them, which in turn shifts your approach to the sales process. If your approach is off, you could crash and burn.

Each hack is explained in a three to five minute video. They will invite you to see things in a simple, and neutral way that makes you instantly more effective at selling your product or service. There are no beginning points or ending points to the hacks. They are designed around what you feel is holding you back or getting in *your* way in the sales process. Even my mom, who is afraid to pick up the phone to make a sales call, while watching these videos was nodding in agreement, saying, "Yep! That's exactly how it feels." Love you, Mom. That was all the proof I needed.

My wish is that you enjoy what I have to share with you and gain value for yourself as so many of my friends, loved ones, and co-workers have.

BENJAMIN CHATSON, originally from Ohio, currently resides in South Florida. He earned his bachelor's degree in electronics, and for twelve years, he worked as an outside technician and expert trouble shooter for AT&T. Well traveled in different personal development arenas, he has invested thousands of volunteer hours as a trainer and a coach with multiple organizations. In June 2016 he attained his trainer certification with Trainer Designs Global. Benjamin made his way into sales five years ago. What he discovered was that it was actually himself that made the job, not the other way around.

Benjamin has been producing consistently stellar results with ease as a sales professional for an extended period of more than a few years. His approach is very simple for people to grasp. He also has a passion for consulting with entrepreneurs and businesses on how they can improve and develop their mind-set regarding sales as well as their work environments in order to maximize potential and improve results.

As a mentor, Benjamin freely shares information on sales, relationships, and mind-set management.

WORK IT!

Deirdre Virvo

It dawned on me one day, about a dozen years ago, that I wanted to be a full-time real estate investor. I used to invest back when I had oodles of extra money and a very profitable business that provided steady income. But twelve years ago I had precisely the opposite. I had no income, an upside-down business, and *less* than no money. What I did have was $1.5 million dollars of debt, a high monthly personal family overhead, and three kids in college. I needed money. First to buy food, then pay the utilities, mortgage, gas, and then pay for ten more years of college tuition. After that the money would go to pay back the debt I had accumulated, then replenish my depleted pension and savings plans . . . the list went on and on. It seemed endless.

It looked like I would be able to invest after I earned my next three million dollars—and that looked like about the twelfth of NEVER.

I decided *never* was too far away and I would just start investing *that* day.

That's what I did—and I have never looked back.

Weighing my options: I decided that I could wallow in loss and self-pity and be broke, or I could shift my direction and set my sights toward success. Being financially strapped was totally exhausting. Boy, was I tired of being tired. I decided to expend my energy by learning a new field, climbing out of debt, and helping my family live the lifestyle they were accustomed to and deserved. We had grown used to traveling the world, throwing epic parties, helping others financially, and being carefree when it came to spending. Time to laser-focus on my new career.

Investing in real estate was an exhilarating and exciting adventure for me. In my past life, I was a realtor's dream—paying full asking price for investment properties, never negotiating, and bringing money to the bank to help pay the monthly mortgages when tenants' rents did not cover them. Investing for the accelerated tax depreciation and the hopeful upside of appreciation.

Now, with my life totally different, I had to learn to invest differently. Creativity and figuring out how to buy real estate without my own money or credit was what was needed. Monthly rental income and appreciation were key. In other words: I needed the cash so everything needed to immediately cash flow!

Luckily, there are a plethora of classes and mentors on the topic of investing. I wanted to study it all—I drank in the knowledge, read all the books, and took classes from all the masters. Enthralled with the endless world of investing possibilities that were at my feet! I learned about wholesaling, rehabbing, apartment house buying, note buying, trusts, self-directed IRAs, appraising, commercial investing, self-storage investing—and then I took a weekend-long seminar on short-saling. Short saling involved helping people get out from under upside-down mortgages. It required patience, finesse, good math skills, and no capital (all of which I had and didn't have). I would be providing a major service for people in dire need, which spoke to my inner social worker's soul *and* making money . . . which spoke to my need to pay bills and do the best for my family.

My decision was made: I was going to negotiate short sales. The housing market had just crashed; there was a huge need for short-sale negotiating. But how would I get clients? How would I tell people what I do when I hadn't actually ever done it? Sales was never something I was very comfortable with. Yet I needed business; I desperately needed to make money for my family.

One Monday morning I made a pact with myself to tell everyone I met that day about my short sale services, no matter how uncomfortable that felt to me. At 9:00 a.m. I ran an errand to the post office. True to my word, I sheepishly told the post office counter person that I helped people get out of trouble with their mortgages and told her that if she knew of anyone who needed a short sale, they could call me. I passed her my very first. freshly printed. short sale business card and got ready to bolt out of embarrassment. She asked me if I would wait a few minutes while she served the long line of post office customers behind me.

When she finally came out to the main lobby she confided that she herself needed my services! Wow. That provided me with the confidence to let others know. Soon thereafter I was conducting presentations and teaching short sales at real estate offices, lawyer's offices, and churches. I rented space and started advertising my own classes. In no time, I was not just a short sale negotiator—I had become the go-to expert, the queen of short sales in Connecticut, successfully negotiating more than one hundred short sales per year! Being tenacious empowered me to close even the toughest of deals. I was crazy busy and making good money. I was working it.

From that day on, I've never shied away from spreading the word about what I do. I know with confidence that I am helping others. It is one of my life's purposes.

Once I mastered short-saling, I started adding to my investing skills: buying apartment buildings, wholesaling, and flipping houses.

After taking a weekend seminar in rehabbing from two brilliant young guys who were rehabbing homes in New Haven, Connecticut. Now, ten years later, they have a hugely successful nationwide seminar and investment business known as FortuneBuilders. They told us that they found employees by looking for smart, hungry, people that could work within their system. That gave me an idea. There was a young college grad who persistently called me, asking endless questions about investing. We had met the month earlier when I had taught a class on grassroots investing at a local real estate school where he was one of the students.

In my past life, I had been the co-owner of a twenty-five-person ad agency, and I knew about leverage. So there I was late at night, after a long seminar, emailing this Realtor student, asking him if he wanted to be my free intern. He immediately emailed his enthusiastic reply, "Yes, I will be there at 8:00 a.m.!" I immediately replied, "Great, come at 10:00 a.m.—I work from home." Two can do exponentially more business than double that of one. In less than one year, he became my full business partner. That was ten years ago.

My partner and I have since grown the business, adding a team of realtors along with starting the SoCT Real Estate Investor Association, an affiliate of the National REIA, in an effort to learn from those more accomplished, network with like-minded investors, and grow more profitable faster.

Once we amassed real estate knowledge, we added personal transformation and growth to our repertoire; we took classes at Landmark Education and the Tony Robbins Institute as well as being coached by Tom Ferry and Paul Finck.

Getting out of debt, helping others, and creating the beginnings of wealth have brought me admiration in my children's eyes—not to mention great soirees and numerable, fabulous travel adventures! When my kids comment on my drive and ever-positive attitude and ask me about work, I tell them, "I'm not working—I'm working it!"

DEIRDRE JP VIRVO is the founding member and co-owner of CT Property Network and SoCT Real Estate Investor Association. She started investing in rental properties a few months after purchasing her own home at the tender age of twenty-three. Deirdre is a seasoned investor as well as a licensed debt negotiator and certified distressed property expert. She teaches grassroots investing techniques throughout Connecticut.

A former advertising VP and ad agency owner for fifteen years, Deirdre pursued full-time investing and founded CT Property Network, a company that specializes in negotiating short sales, renovating and flipping houses, and acquiring and holding residential and commercial buildings. Education, networking, and empowerment form the foundation of SoCT REIA, which she created out of her desire to network and learn from other real estate investors in her area.

Deirdre, a native New Yorker, resides in Stamford with her beau, Chris Sinatra. She has three fabulous adult children (who have started investing in real estate) and three school-age stepchildren. Going to the theatre, entertaining, traveling, dancing, crafting, teaching, volunteering, and helping others are among her passions. Deirdre credits her upbeat spirit and love for life to her family and her loving parents, and to being a big fan of Landmark Education and Tony Robbins.

FROM FINANCIAL RUIN TO BUSINESS SUCCESS

Dr. Teresa R. Martin, ESQ

My journey from financial ruin to business success was a long one, beginning in 2001.

As a highly paid corporate attorney, the world was my oyster. My legal career took me to the New York City Law Department where I worked on litigation cases for NYPD and things of that sort. My world was turned upside down on that fateful day of 9/11/2001 when the World Trade Center was attacked. My office was one block from that attack.

The devastation of this one incident changed my life. The attacks left me jobless for months, my home went into foreclosure, my truck was repossessed, and I was forced into a Chapter 13 bankruptcy filing through a pro se action.

I'd heard about how difficult the foreclosure process could be for those who encounter sudden economic downfalls. The loss of a job or a drop in salary can easily cause a family to lose their home. While this is a hard situation for these families, it creates countless opportunities for others. Was I now one of these statistics?

Here I was, a one-time corporate attorney with a very impressive financial portfolio who was now being forced into financial desperation to save my home from foreclosure. I embraced my inner strength. I learned bankruptcy and foreclosure law. I fought for my home, my family, and my dignity.

As a result, the bankruptcy was dismissed. The lender allowed me to sell my home, and I even received a large profit from that situation. After this humbling experience, I finally understood my purpose. I was not meant to end my journey as a corporate attorney, and that journey definitely wasn't to allow me to build up my storehouses on this earth. My journey was to withstand the test and to empower others to do the same.

The mortgage meltdown didn't start until late 2007 to 2008. I emerged from my situation and became a real estate, bankruptcy, and foreclosure defense attorney with a special focus on helping others to build wealth through real estate.

When stress is thrown your way, the only thing you can control is your reaction to it. The better you get at controlling your reactions, the more resilient you'll be, and the more likely you'll be able to transform a bad situation into a positive one.

Stress provides the body with energy. That energy tends to be spent worrying or feeling anxious, but what if you could use that energy for good? You'd be able to transform that negative, nervous energy into positive outlets that improve your life!

Bankruptcy isn't the answer for everyone, because each individual circumstance is different. It isn't a cure-all that will make all your financial issues go away. With that in mind, bankruptcy may be your best option. With expert help, you can decide if it's the best fit for your circumstances.

I went from losing one home to now having a large real estate portfolio, and I have developed the ability to help others to achieve their dreams of home ownership, financial security, and business ownership. I help people to build generational wealth instead of generational poverty. Real estate and financial empowerment is now my ministry, and I love it.

All in all, I'm pretty happy with how my business turned out despite the financial obstacles. I've built a solid foundation to support even more growth, and I've managed to create a business and lifestyle by design.

If you are someone who actually desire, despite your financial resources, to become an entrepreneur, my advice is to know what you do and do what you know. Don't start a business simply because it seems sexy or it boosts large hypothetical profit margins and returns.

Do what you love. Businesses are built around your strengths and talents. You will have a greater chance of success if you do what you love. It's not only important to create a profitable business; it's also important that you're happy managing and growing it day in and day out. If your heart isn't in it, then you won't be successful.

No business book or no business plan can predict the future or fully prepare you to become a successful entrepreneur. There is no such thing as a perfect plan. There is no perfect road. So you should never jump right into a new business without any thought or planning, but don't spend months or years waiting to execute your plan either.

As a former attorney who has struggled to build my real estate and business coaching service, I'd like to take a moment to share five concepts I attribute to my success that has multiplied my business exponentially.

1. Create a Powerful Vision. Having a strong vision for your business is important and can represent the deciding moment you. Not knowing where you need to be spells calamity! Making an big vision for where you need to be in three years, one year, and thirty days in your business encourages you to stay focused on what is essential.

2. Participate in Workshops. This one is huge. Nothing beats escaping your office and getting away from your PC to meet individuals in person. I've left these learning events having gained customers, joint venture partners, and immense data I was able to retain and put to use in both my business and my clients' organizations.

3. Contract a Mentor. In the past, I didn't have formalized mentors, and everything I learned came from someone who has done it before. Contracting with a mentor was a difficult choice to make; however, I'm truly happy I did. It's hard to see your business dispassionately, so having an impartial advisor on your team is highly important. Mentors enable you to escape your own less-productive habits and get out of your own way. They can help you with both your internal game (your propensities and outlook) and your external game (your abilities and business structure).

4. Systemize Your Business. Unless you want to be shackled to your business night and day, you must begin systemizing your business. Truly, all organizations ought to have frameworks and systems set up—even if you are a solo-professional. The best part is that when you do have frameworks and systems set up, your business suddenly begins running significantly more productively and successfully (and you can begin resting more and working less).

5. Outsource Your Weakness. For all you control freaks out there, this one is for you. Outsourcing means transferring some portion of your business's work to an outside service provider instead of doing it internally. When done right, outsourcing is a valuable, cost-saving measure that makes your company more efficient. If you don't start hiring some help, I guarantee you'll never be able to grow your business because you'll be constantly doing tasks you have no business doing.

You'll only become a well-rounded entrepreneur when you're tested under fire. The most important thing that you can do is to learn from your mistakes and never make the same mistake twice.

The lack of finances or lack of resources has never stopped anyone from doing anything. If you have the will and the determination, you can do anything that you set your mind to do. In my opinion, there is no such thing as "self-made" millionaires—only "team-made" millionaires. If you don't have the finances, networking can put you in places where you can meet someone who does. If you don't have the credit, you can be put into a situation where somebody can help you to improve your credit or even rent their credit to you while you rebuild your credit.

There are so many different things you can do to be successful, and it's not necessarily about profits.

My goal is to help five thousand families achieve financial security, affecting five generations in five years within my network. I created Generational Wealth Zone to act as a catalyst in creating generational wealth by breaking the chains of generational poverty affecting five thousand families, one family at a time.

My best advice to entrepreneurs is to learn from my journey from financial ruin to business success. I hope I have encouraged you to join the challenge and change the trajectory of your legacy.

Be Fiscally Fabulous!

DR. TERESA R. MARTIN, ESQ, is a motivational speaker, author, million-dollar real estate wealth coach, business strategist, and legal counsel. She is living the life she loves and can teach you how to do the same!

As founder of the Generational Wealth Zone Group, Teresa Martin formed the original vision for a group of companies that would help clients create, manage, protect, and grow their wealth. She is dedicated to showing individuals and entrepreneurs how to become financially empowered by turning the work they love into a profitable and sustainable business.

Aside from being a successful attorney and founder of Generational Wealth Zone, Teresa is also a well-seasoned real estate investor who focuses on the creative acquisition strategies she has developed, implemented, and taught to others through the Real Estate Investors Association NYC (REIA NYC).

Teresa is an expert about talking openly about all things money—how to ask for money, how to track money, and how to make more money!

She continues to shape the Generational Wealth Zone vision today, providing the energy and inspiration to continually move the company forward to greater achievements for her clients.

See all our authors:

BeASuccessMaverick.com

Join TMMP Maverick Authors' Family
with a book of your own:

TheMaverickMillionairePublishing.com

9 780999 638156